Stalin Versus Marx

Stalin Versus Marx

THE STALINIST HISTORICAL DOCTRINE

BY

KLAUS MEHNERT

TRANSLATED
FROM THE GERMAN

KENNIKAT PRESS
Port Washington, N. Y./London

STALIN VERSUS MARX

First published in 1952
Reissued in 1972 by Kennikat Press
Library of Congress Catalog Card No: 77-159093
ISBN 0-8046-1636-1

Manufactured by Taylor Publishing Company   Dallas, Texas

TO MY DEAD FRIEND MICHAEL

Talks at night in Shanghai
during the long winter of Stalingrad
laid the foundation for this essay

Foreword

Some time ago a friend, a student of history, sent me the German language edition of a Soviet Russian historical work by Professor A. M. Pankratova. He had found that book, he wrote, extremely surprising. The book was called *History of the U.S.S.R.*, and he expected to find in it the history of the Soviet Union since 1917, or, perhaps, since the founding of the Bolshevik party in 1903; but the book began with the Assyrians and Chaldeans. He had never, he said, met with anything madder.

He was perfectly right. The first pages of this *History of the U.S.S.R.*, contain such passages as these:

"In the middle of the second millennium B.O.E." (before our era, i.e. B.C., but the author wished to avoid any reference to Christ), "there lived . . . by the upper waters of the rivers Tigris and Euphrates, whose sources are in the Caucasus, and by their tributaries, little groups of tribes. They were exposed to frequent attacks from the Assyrian kings. . . . At the beginning of the first millennium B.O.E. the tribal groups amalgamated. They acquired the name of Chaldeans, from their god Khald. . . . At the end of the eighth century B.O.E. the power of that State began to diminish markedly. In the north the Chaldeans were harassed by nomads. On the Tigris, Assyria once more became a powerful State. . . . In the middle of the sixth century B.O.E. the Persian kingdom in the south-east grew in strength. The fighting with Persia weakened the Chaldean tribes. . . ."

Between the nineteen-twenties, in which a *History of the U.S.S.R* would begin with the Bolshevik Revolution, or, if it was ambitious, with a few precursors of the Bolsheviks, and the forties, in which a *History of the U.S.S.R.* began with the history of ancient Mesopotamia, a change had taken place in Bolshevik thought, a change of which the significance extends far beyond the field of the teaching of history, and which may supply a key, perhaps *the* key, to the understanding of present-day Bolshevism.

Contents

*

I

Pokrovsky Died Twice

*

A new period in Soviet historiography began on
May 16th, 1934. On that day Stalin and Molotov
signed a decree concerning the teaching of history,
which was to introduce a new Bolshevik ideology
diametrically opposed to the earlier one. On that day
Pokrovsky died a second death.

I first met Michael N. Pokrovsky, who was a
prominent Russian historian, in Moscow in 1930. At
that time I was collecting material for a study of Soviet
universities, and Pokrovsky held a leading position in
Soviet cultural administration. A son of the old Tsarist
Russia, he had gone over to the Bolshevik Revolution
in 1905; after years of *émigré* life he had returned to
Russia in August 1917 and had energetically collabo-
rated in Lenin's revolution. He soon became chairman
of the Moscow soviet—the chief of all the soviets—
and ultimately he was elected to the Central Committee
of the party.

I found in him no proletarian labour leader, but,
behind his horn-rimmed spectacles, a typical Russian
professor. He was then at the summit of his career,
holding a number of important posts. His *History of
Russia*, written before the First World War, had been
published in a huge edition, and was to be found in
every library in the country and in many abroad. The

work was then the bible of every Soviet historian;
Lenin, too, had given it his blessing, writing to Pokrovsky: "I congratulate you very heartily on your success.
I like your new *History of Russia* enormously. It is
original in its construction and exposition. It makes
most interesting reading. In my opinion it ought to be
translated into the European languages."

When, in 1932, Pokrovsky died, he was given a State
funeral, with military honours, in the Red Square in
Moscow, and his ashes were placed in the wall of the
Kremlin, not far from the Lenin Mausoleum. In
countless commemorative articles it was declared that
in him the Soviet Union had lost a faithful disciple of
Marx and Lenin and a great Bolshevik.

The decree of May 16th, 1934, completely reversed
all that. Pokrovsky's achievement, and the Pokrovsky
school, were condemned root and branch. A flood of
newspaper articles followed, in which Pokrovsky's
disciples were described as "enemies of the people and
contemptible Trotskyist agents of Fascism". A similar
fate befell many other old militants among the
Bolsheviks in the years that followed, but that happened
in their lifetime or after their "liquidation". For a man
who, two full years after his death, was still regarded
with the utmost veneration, to be suddenly denounced
as an enemy of his country, was a thing unprecedented
even in the Soviet Union. In order finally to dispose of
Pokrovsky, and to trample him to death a second time
in his grave, the Moscow Academy of Sciences published in 1939 a volume *Against M. N. Pokrovsky's
Historical Conception*, in whose 500-odd pages a series of
articles set out to annihilate Pokrovsky. And while

the dead historian's star was thus fading out in the black night of excommunication, another star began to shine brightly, that of his colleague Eugene Tarle. As recently as 1931, Tarle had been violently attacked in the *Borba Klassov*, the organ of the Marxist historians, as "a Russian bourgeois historian, an imperialist, a chauvinist of the First World War, an ideological torch bearer of the imperialist front directed against the Soviet Union". By 1934 Tarle had become one of the leading historians of the Soviet Union, and long articles of his on important questions of world politics appeared at frequent intervals in the Moscow national newspapers.

What was the reason for this upheaval?

TASKS OF THE SOVIET HISTORIAN UNTIL 1934

Pokrovsky's task in writing his history was the same which—until 1934—every Soviet historian had to face: to demonstrate, through the example of the history of any and every nation at any and every period (in Pokrovsky's case, through the example of Russian history), the truth of Marx's "historical materialism". To the Bolsheviks of that time history was of interest only in so far as it illustrated Marx's theories. The writing of history was nothing else than an application of the "iron law of history" laid down by Marx. Pokrovsky had nobly fulfilled that task. What he describes in his history is thus not so much the Russian as the universal element.

Another task of the Soviet historians before 1934 had been to depict the Soviet Union in glowing colours; this was the easier the darker the picture of pre-1917 Russia was drawn. Pre-revolutionary Russia as painted by the Pokrovsky school resembles a prison in which the peoples languished under the brutal cruelty of Tsarist oppression. For two centuries the Russian intellectuals had been divided on the question whether the Russians belonged to the West or to a culture of their own; but that question did not interest Pokrovsky. He was equally contemptuous of the capitalist West and of the imperialist dreams of the Slavophils. In his view, day first dawned for mankind with the Bolshevik Revolution. Such was the official version of history in the Soviet Union until the decree of 1934.

We will not reproduce the decree of May 16th, 1934. Apart from its condemnation of the Soviet historiography of the past, it contains little of importance, and in any case nothing that might indicate the direction that would be taken by future Soviet historians. I must admit that at the time I did not realise the full significance of the decree. I associated it to some extent with the Soviet patriotism of which the first signs were becoming visible, but it was not until a decade later that I discovered the deeper meaning of the decree. In wage policy, or in legislation on family life, it is possible to see at once how the course has been changed; but even in the Soviet Union it takes years for a newly established historical doctrine to be elaborated. The real meaning of the volte-face of 1934 has never been publicly formulated by the Soviets themselves. But it can be clearly reconstructed with the aid of the historical works compiled in the nineteen-thirties and published in the forties. In this case, as so often, the observer of the Soviet Union must patiently assemble his facts and then seek the reasons to which they owe their appearance. I cannot vouch for the accuracy of my interpretation; but it sets forth a hypothesis and one for which there is the backing of a large measure of probability, and which renders intelligible many circumstances that without it are difficult to explain.

SOVIET UNION AS QUINTESSENCE OF MANKIND

It seems to us that the development of the Soviet Union since 1917 had destroyed the credibility of Marx's presentation of history (on which Pokrovsky relied) in five respects. To begin with the Revolution contradicted the Marxist forecast (see, for example, the Communist Manifesto) by breaking out not in a number of advanced countries but in a single backward one, Russia. (The country that followed, 32 years later —China—was still more backward.) The Bolsheviks accordingly elaborated a "law of the uneven development of capitalism in the age of imperialism". (As Marx lived before the age of imperialism, there was no need to blame him for ignorance of that law.) Inasmuch as the Soviet State founded in 1917 was the only full representative of the Socialism prophesied by Marx, it became of independent value. Something that was particular (the Soviet Union) now represented something that was general (mankind), and so the particular became of more importance than the general—the exact opposite of Pokrovsky's basic conception. Moreover, the Soviet State had proceeded from the Russian State. From the new rôle that fell to the Soviet State, the old pre-1917 Russian State and its history acquired new importance. Since the particular (the Soviet Union) had become the quintessence of mankind, Soviet history (and therefore Russian history in general), was bound to become the quintessence of human history. So the men of the Kremlin saw the matter.

TO EACH ACCORDING TO HIS ACHIEVEMENT

Secondly, Marx had taught that Man's consciousness is determined by his social existence, that is to say by the material conditions under which he lives. That being so, so fundamental a change in the environment as that which the victory of Bolshevism had entailed ought to have led to a corresponding change in human consciousness and human nature. It was anticipated, for example, that the socialisation of property, which in theory made all citizens joint owners of the whole of the national property, would bring with it a new attitude to work—that the workers, who in the past had worked with no particular will, simply for the sake of their wages, for an owner who was nothing to them, would now be working for themselves and therefore with incomparably greater energy and success. Yet nothing of the sort happened. Many workers' output was poorer at first than under capitalism. For more than a decade, production remained far below that of the years before 1917; indeed, the workers had to be induced to work by a vast amount of police measures, and, from June 1931, by a piece-work system which was soon pushed to the uttermost extreme, providing a little extra pay for every little bit of extra work. The principle of payment by results was thus given immense importance, entirely against the expectation of the old Bolsheviks. That principle of payment had been an essential element of the capitalist system. If payment by results was to be made the central principle of Soviet industrial policy, it could no longer be maintained that the Soviet economic system differed from the capitalist system as day from night. Instead, a new doctrine was elaborated; it was based on a section, to which little attention had been paid until then, of Marx's *Critique of the Gotha Programme* (1875). According to the new doctrine, the first system to succeed the capitalist economic system was Socialism, a system related to capitalism in so far as it retained payment by results. This idea was incorporated in the new Soviet Constitution in 1936: "In the U.S.S.R. is realised the fundamental principle of Socialism, 'From each according to his capacity; to each according to his work'." (Article 12.)

Only later—when, no one has said—is there to emerge from the Socialist economy the Communist one, which is supposed to be able to dispense with payment by results. Only then will the Communist principle rule, "To each according to his needs". The conception from which Pokrovsky had proceeded, that Socialism is the entire opposite, the antithesis, of capitalism, was dropped.

GOD IS NOT YET DEAD

Thirdly, in Marx's line of thought religion was one of the components of the "social consciousness", which, after the achievement of the Revolution and the transformation of the forces of production, would quickly begin to disappear. For Pokrovsky, too, Christianity, like all religion, was an unqualified evil.

After the Revolution, however, it was found that religion was much more deeply rooted in the Russian people than had been supposed. In 1936 the poet Demyan Bedny, "singer of the proletariat", was severely reprimanded for his mockery of Christianity; the reprimand made it clear that from then on the Christianisation of the early Russia was to be officially regarded as having exerted "a progressive influence". A few years later, during the Second World War, a close alliance was concluded between the State and the loyal hierarchy of the Church.

THE STATE DID NOT DIE, AND THE PROLETARIANS DID NOT UNITE

Fourthly, according to Marx the State would die away after the Revolution. Its place was to be taken by the free association of people. In reality the Bolshevik State showed no sign of preparing to die; on the contrary, it became more powerful every year, and incomparably more powerful than the Tsarist State had ever been. Thus, on this point, too, the Soviet Union was not, as Pokrovsky had represented it, the antipodes of the Tsardom.

No one recognised this more clearly than Stalin. But it is impossible to praise the Bolshevik State and at the same time utterly condemn the Tsardom when the two are in many respects—even in banishments to Siberia—identical.

Fifthly, for Marx "the proletariat" was the decisive

force in modern history. Nations, in his view, were already moribund. ("The workers have no country." Comm. Manifesto.) But during and after the First World War the nations had shown themselves to be an uncommonly live force, and had shown such cohesion that the summons so persuasively uttered by Marx, "Proletarians of all countries, unite!", was reduced to an anaemic theory. Not only that, but there had risen between proletariat and bourgeoisie, alongside the old middle class which Marx had described as dying, an entirely new middle class which had hardly existed at the time of the Communist Manifesto. This new middle class, made up of technicians, engineers, officials, scientists, business managers, and so on, belonged neither to Marx's bourgeoisie (since it consists of employees) nor (although it consists of employees) to Marx's proletariat; and it had acquired an importance entirely unforeseen by Marx. It soon became clear that even in the Soviet Union the proletariat was far from assuming leadership; power fell very quickly into the hands of the "managers". The word "proletariat" fell more and more out of use, ousted first by the word "toilers", a much more comprehensive term, and then by "the people". Everybody who reads Communist newspapers knows how rarely one meets with the term "proletarians" in them. In Soviet publicity, too, it has almost disappeared, except—as a matter of tradition— at the head of the newspapers in the slogan "Proletarians of all countries, unite!" The moment the faith in the "proletarians of all countries" disappeared, the old presentation of history furnished by Pokrovsky was bound to give place to a new one.

These disappointments in face of Marx's prophecies and theses explain the changed purpose of the Soviet historical doctrine since the beginning of the thirties. While Pokrovsky was presenting Marx's "iron laws" in the almost fortuitous example of Russia, the aim of the new historical doctrine is to explain why the Revolution succeeded in Russia of all countries. But if that was to be explained, the roots of the Soviet State and of its history had to be sought in the history of the Russian people and State, with the resulting emergence of a totally different valuation of Russian history from that furnished by Pokrovsky.

II

Two Words Vindicated

*

The aim of Stalin's historical doctrine was thus the opposite of that of Pokrovsky's time.

There remains the question why the radical change in the historical doctrine came when it did in the spring of 1934. The answer is perhaps revealed if we take into consideration a number of events that took place just then, within a space of five weeks.

On May 16th, 1934, Stalin signed the decree already mentioned, introducing an entire revaluation of world history.

On June 8th the Central Executive Committee of the U.S.S.R. promulgated a "Law on the Betrayal of the Country", imposing the heaviest penalties, not only on offenders but on members of their families who were not involved, for espionage, the betrayal of military secrets or secrets of state, and similar crimes. In that decree there appeared once more the word *rodina* (fatherland), which had long been taboo.

On June 9th the Moscow *Pravda* published a leading article on patriotism, in which the word "patriot", which had also been barred for many years, was restored to honour. The leading article summoned all Soviet citizens "to the struggle for the fatherland, for its honour, fame, power, and prosperity", and worked up to this climax: "The defence of the fatherland is the supreme law of life". This was surprising language. The word "fatherland" is but an inadequate rendering of *rodina*. The fatherland may be a chosen abode. *Rodina* contains the same root as the word *rodit'*, "to give birth". *Rodina* is the country that gave birth to us, the country with which our destiny is bound up, not by chance or on account of economic considerations but by the ties of blood. The Bolsheviks had spoken of the Soviet Union in the past as the "fatherland of the workers" or the "Socialist fatherland". But in using the word "fatherland" only with qualifications, only in association with other words, they had deliberately weakened it. Now it suddenly came out in full force— *rodina*.

BACK FROM THE ICEBERG

Ten days later, on June 19th, 1934, there took place on the Red Square in Moscow the ceremony of welcoming the Russians who had set out in the "Chelyuskin" for the Polar region of the Arctic Ocean and ultimately, after abandoning their ship and spending weeks of hardship on an iceberg, had been rescued by Soviet aviators without loss of life. The whole incident had unquestionably made great demands on the endurance and will-power of the crew and the aviators. But the reception prepared for them went far beyond anything justified by the achievement in itself. If in a country in which human lives are not dealt with too tenderly, the rescue of 104 people taken off an iceberg was turned, after an intensive press campaign carried on for weeks, into a demonstration attended by millions, the reason was simply that the men at the head of the State had decided that the event was a suitable occasion for the first patriotic celebration in the Soviet State.

When on that June day at about 5.30 p.m., I entered the press stand, next to the Lenin Mausoleum, the Red Square was already covered by tens of thousands of soldiers of the Red Army, members of the Comsomol (the Communist youth organisation), and members of sports groups, in serried ranks. Along the far side of the Red Square hung gigantic portraits of Lenin and Stalin, flanked by portraits of the seven airmen and the leading members of the ship's company. At the left end of the Square, on the wall of the Historical Museum, an immense map had been set up to show the course of the "Chelyuskin" off the coast of Siberia. On the right, near the famous Church of Saint Basil, with its many fantastically coloured domes, on the site of the former place of execution, stood a vast papier-mâché iceberg, with an almost full-size model of the "Chelyuskin".

Soon after six o'clock came a sort of floral procession —fifty cars, covered with peonies, bringing the heroes of the day, welcomed with the acclamations of the crowd and the long-drawn-out hurrahs of the soldiers, shouted from end to end of the Square. They took their places on a special platform. Now Stalin came from the Kremlin, accompanied by his closest colleagues, through the Nikolsky Gate. Then the orations began, all praising the men of the "Chelyuskin" as patriots who had done all this out of love for their country; and then came an ovation for *Velikyi Stalin*—Stalin the Great. A parade of the troops followed, with manœuvring of tanks and aircraft, and, finally, long after dark, a procession of the people of Moscow, mustered district by district, with red flags and slogans and transparencies showing the leaders and the men of the "Chelyuskin", and with bands and singing and bursts of cheering.

I had often witnessed these parades on the Red Square—on November 7th, the anniversary of the Bolshevik victory, and on May Day; but on that nineteenth of June one felt that this was a celebration of another sort, newer—or, rather, primeval. For some years, it is true, this new element was not often at the front of the stage, but it continued to grow in the background and out of sight. Years later it was to show its strength at Stalingrad.

HITLER'S INFLUENCE

Taken together, these events, which took place in Moscow between May 16th and June 19th, 1934, may give the answer to the question why the reversal of the Bolshevik historical doctrine took place just at that time. The victory of National Socialism in Germany had given a severe shock to the leaders of the Soviet State. In the Kremlin, as in many other places in the world, it had at first been hoped and expected that that event would be no more than a flash in the pan. But month after month Hitler's position had become stronger instead of weaker. A year had now passed since he came to power, and it was realised that the prospect must be faced of the endurance of the Hitler régime for a considerable period. It was recognised that Hitler's nationalism had revealed in Germany a driving force beyond all comparison with Thälmann's Marxism. The fate of Germany was a matter of primary importance in

24

the strategic calculations of the Bolshevik leaders, and consequently there could no longer be any escape from a complete change in the policy of the Kremlin. If Bolshevism was not to be allowed to fall seriously behind in the struggle of the world ideologies, the nationalist outlook must become a central instead of an incidental element of Bolshevik thought. The victory of Nazism in Germany, together with a series of setbacks in the U.S.S.R., especially the serious agricultural situation in 1931–33, with the widespread famine resulting from collectivisation, had compelled Bolshevism to re-examine its position. There could no longer be any expectation of the world revolution within a measurable time. On what or on whom, then, should Stalin base his new world policy? On whom else than the peoples of the Soviet Union, and primarily the Russians?

So came the great *volte-face*, the rediscovery of *rodina* and of patriotism. The new position naturally had to be given an ideology of its own. The task of creating that ideology was entrusted to the Soviet historians.

III

The New Doctrine

*

We know, then, the reason for the revision of the picture of Russian history. Our next question is, In what does the Stalinist picture of that history essentially consist?

At this point let us return for a moment to the outset of this essay, to the fact that a "History of the U.S.S.R." begins with the Chaldeans and Assyrians. How can that be possible? The answer is quite simple. For the present-day Soviet historian everything that ever happened within the present-day boundaries of the U.S.S.R. is a part of Soviet history. This very simple contention discards the whole of the past treatment of history—not only of the Soviet Union but of Russia—and opens up to the Soviet historian a wide field of opportunity and one, as will be shown, of importance to international politics.

It results to begin with in an immense extension of "Soviet history", an extension both in time and in space. In a recent work of Soviet historiography Professor Pankratova, author of the *History of the U.S.S.R.* already referred to, writes: "Stalin extended the limits of the period of Soviet history by 1500 to 2000 years." This is not a joke but an entirely serious statement. The view adopted, whether by Stalin himself or with his consent, that Soviet history is to be regarded as equivalent to the history of the present territory of the Soviet Union, makes the archaeological discoveries in Transcaucasia and central Asia, regions very close to the cradle of the history of mankind, elements of Soviet history. Thus regarded, Soviet history begins in the third millennium "before our era", with the discovery of the oldest copper articles in the mountains of the Caucasus.

The new definition of "Soviet History" enormously extends not only its limits in time but its geographical limits, for it automatically brings into Soviet history not only everything that has ever been brought to light at any time in the regions of the present U.S.S.R., but also the interconnexion of these events with other parts of the world. We have seen this already in the case of the Assyrians. Very useful in this connexion are the Scythians, to whom further reference will be made, and the Caucasian peoples. Professors S. V. Kisselyov, V. I. Avdiev, and M. A. Korostovtsev have discovered that in early times the Caucasian races had close relations with all the ancient cultures of the Middle East, even with that of Egypt. The relations of the races of central Asia belonging today to the Soviet Union, some of which were subjugated by the Tsarist legions no more than a few centuries ago, opened the doors for the Soviets to the whole history of Asia. Professor A. Okladnikov offers evidence of close relations between the Yakuts of north-east Siberia with China actually in the bronze age, and through Alaska, which belonged for some decades to Russia, run threads to the history of America, while Russian voyages of discovery connect Soviet history with the South Pole.

The first essential trait of the new Soviet historical

doctrine was thus a matter of form, namely the extension in time and space of what is to be understood as Soviet history. The second and yet more important trait is to be seen in its content. It has reference to the new attitude of Bolshevism to the nation. For the Russian people the great importance of the nation is no new idea; it has led the popular prophets to preach again and again in the past the special mission of the Russians. This messianic conception of the nation is new, however, in the realm of Marxism. To Marx, and also to Pokrovsky, nations were not intrinsically of importance, and when the Bolsheviks—including Stalin in his earlier writings—paid some attention to the characteristics of peoples it was only in order the more quickly to give the influence of Bolshevism access to them through concessions to the formal elements of their national culture—language, popular music, and so on. The present conception of the nation, or, at all events, of the Soviet nation, is distinguished fundamentally, as we shall see, from that of Marx and Pokrovsky and their contemporaries of like mind. From this proceeds a whole chain of consequences, which we will pursue throughout its twelve links.

To avoid misunderstanding, it should be mentioned that the twelve stages through which we shall trace the development of the Soviet historiographical conception are links in thought and not in time. The series 1–12 is a logical series, independent of the time when each link in the chain of thought became visible to the public. Thus, the transformation in the field of philology, here logically given fourth place, would belong in time to the last place. The intrinsic interconnexion of this whole train of thought has never been discovered by the Soviets. They will also emphatically reject the contention in this essay that such an intrinsic inter-connexion exists.

1. THE PEOPLES ARE VARIOUS AND ETERNAL

It has become clear again and again from Stalin's statements and actions that he regards the peoples as differing from one another—not only in their stage of development but also in their nature. He gave the clearest expression to this idea in a speech on April 7th, 1948, during a banquet in honour of a Finnish delegation:

"Many people do not believe that it is possible for the relations between greater and lesser peoples to be on a basis of equality of rights. But we of the Soviet are of the opinion that every people, whether great or small, has its qualitative characteristics, its individuality, which is its own possession and is not to be found in other peoples. These characteristics are the contribution (*vklad*) which each people brings to the general treasury of world civilisation, filling it and enriching it. In this sense all peoples, small and great alike, are in the same situation."

Nine months earlier, in an address delivered by Professor V. V. Mavrodin in Leningrad, he used, at the very outset, a phrase that revealed, with the utmost clarity and brevity, the completely altered intellectual outlook: "The people is eternal" (*Narod vechen*). The fact that the Society for the Propagation of Political and Scientific Knowledge, a propaganda institution formed a little earlier for the ideological influencing of the population, published this particular address as one of its first mass-produced pamphlets, and gave it the title *The Forming of the Russian Nation*, is proof enough that Mavrodin's phrase was not merely the chance utterance of an individual professor.

It was a truly sensational phrase in a "Marxist" country. What Mavrodin meant by it is shown by his next sentence, which gave the cue to his whole lecture: "Every people, whose name, language, culture, customs, and physical characteristics disappear in the course of time, lives on in the shape of its remote descendants. The primeval races and peoples are the creative force in the formation of later populations and nations."[1]

This doctrine of the variety and eternity of peoples is the basis of the idea of the special position of the Soviet people, and, within the Soviet people, the Russian people.

2. SPECIAL POSITION OF THE SOVIET AND THE RUSSIAN PEOPLE

On May 24th, 1945, there took place in St. George's Hall in the Kremlin, a celebration of victory, at which hundreds of marshals, generals, officers, scientists, engineers, writers, and Stakhanovist workers, were present. As the evening approached its climax, Stalin appeared and proposed the following toast:

"Comrades, permit me to propose one more toast, the last one. I drink to the health of our Soviet people, and quite specially the Russian people. I drink quite

[1] *Phormirovaniye Russkoy Natsyi*, Leningrad 1947, pp. 3-4.

specially to the health of the Russian people because it is the most eminent of all the nations belonging to the federation of the Soviet Union. I drink to the health of the Russian people, because in this war it has earned general recognition as, of all the peoples of our country, the leading element in the Soviet Union. I drink to the health of the Russian people not only because it is a leading people, but also because it has a clear intelligence, a firm character, and endurance. The Russian people has placed faith in the rightness of the policy of its Government, and has made sacrifice to bring about the smashing of Germany. This faith of the Russian people in the Soviet Government has proved to be the decisive force that brought about the victory over the historic enemy of mankind, over Fascism. Thanks be to it, to the Russian people, for that faith! To the health of the Russian people!"

This toast of Stalin's has since become one of the guiding elements of Soviet publicity. On its fifth anniversary the following was to be found in the central organ of the party, the Moscow *Pravda*:

"The Russian people has created the most abundant culture: it has given the world a whole constellation of great scholars, writers, composers, artists, thinkers, and inventors. Russia became the home of Leninism, that peak of the world's science and civilisation. The Russian people gave mankind that thinker of the highest genius, Lenin. . . . The Russian working class has played an eminent rôle in the history of all mankind. It was the first in the world to carry through a soviet revolution, and thereby to institute a new era. . . . The great Soviet Union is today on the march as the

advance guard of the whole of progressive humanity."
(May 24th, 1950.)

It was insisted again and again that the history
of the Soviet people is something special, something
independent of the general current of history. Professor
Rubinstein received a severe reprimand for his work
Russian Historiography because he wrote it from the
point of view of the "cosmopolitan" (which in current
usage is equivalent to "traitorous"), "conception of
a single common current of development in the
historical science of the world, with the result that
Russian historiography is represented as merely a
repetition and a species of all the historical schools and
tendencies that arose in the West and were taken over
later by Russia". Through these views, it was declared,
Rubinstein had brought confusion among the Soviet
historians.[1]

This special position, this leading position of the
Russian people, or the Soviet people and all the
peoples regarded as part of Soviet history, has become a
basic claim of the Soviet historical doctrine. In dealing
with every new publication, therefore, the attention of
critics is directed at once to the question whether
account is duly taken of that claim. Every limitation,
however cautious, however guarded or qualified,
every "belittling" of the Russian people is at once
severely castigated. Here are a few examples:

Against the 'belittlers'

In the historical works of a handful of cosmopolitans
without a homeland, severed from the people and its

[1] *Voprossy Istorii*, 1949, no. 2.

aspirations, free play is being given to a bourgeois cosmopolitanism. The contemporary countryless cosmopolitans are distorting the heroic struggle of the Russian people against its oppressors and the foreign robbers, belittling the leading part played by the Russian proletariat in the history of the revolutionary struggle which it has been carrying on for Russia herself and also for the whole world. They are trying to obliterate the Socialist character and the international significance of the Great Socialist October Revolution; they are falsifying and distorting the world-historic part played by the Russian people in the creation of the Socialist society. . . . In his *History of the Soviet Union, 1917 to 1925*, which has already been subjected to severe criticism in the periodical *Kultura i Zhizn*, the Academician Mints belittles the leading part played by the Russian people and the working class in the struggle for the setting up of Socialist rule. . . . In just the same way Academician Mints, Professor Razgon gives only a one-sided and superficial consideration of history in reducing to very little the leading part played by the Russian people and the Russian working class in the victory of the Great Socialist October Revolution".[1]

For all future historical works the guiding line is: "The task of future research includes the description of the eminent international position and importance of Russia in the system of States."[2]

This amounts to saying that the Soviet historian may only speak of the Russian people in terms of praise. B. Stein, for instance, in his "Sketches of the development of Russian social and economic ideas in the 19th

[1] *Voprossy Istorii*, 1949, no. 2.   [2] *ibid.*, 1949, no. 11, pp. 3 *sqq.*

and 20th centuries", published in 1948 in Leningrad described Russian economists as "talentless and unfitted for independent creative work";[1] for this he was at once castigated.

The most cautious wording does not save an author from attack. Thus, in the official historical journal, F. A. Garin's book, *The Rout of Napoleon* (Moscow 1948), is rejected as unpatriotic. As reason for this the journal reproduces a paragraph from the book. In this Garin quotes a few sentences from the Memoirs of the Comte de Ségur on his impressions of the burning of Moscow. The quotation runs: "Everyone noticed men with repulsive faces, dressed in rags, and furious women, who went past the burning houses and completed the horrible picture of an inferno. These worthless people [Note by Garin: 'In such wild terms did the Napoleonic General Ségur express himself about the patriots of Moscow'], drunk with vodka and with the success of their crimes, did not even conceal themselves." "This wild characterisation of Ségur's", comments Garin, "shows better than anything else the profound hatred felt even by the enlightened among the foreign robbers for the Russian people." In spite of his dissenting comments, the author is set down as anti-patriotic for even quoting such a statement about Russian patriots, although it is clear that he is only doing his duty as a chronicler and does not for a moment identify himself with the Count's views.

[1] *Voprossy Istorii*, 1949, no. 4.

The New Doctrine

3. ETHNOGENESIS—AUTOCHTHONISM—BORROWING

From this attitude of morbidly jealous watching over the special position of the Russian and Soviet people, it becomes clear why three conceptions—ethnogenesis, autochthonism, and borrowing, play an extraordinary part in the vocabulary of the Soviet historians. Whereas earlier Russian historians saw no objection to beginning Russian history no earlier than the time of the foundation of the first State of Kiev in the eighth century, without making it a point of honour to consider what might have happened earlier, the Soviet historians are anxiously concerned to demonstrate, first, that Soviet history began long earlier; second, that it is autochthonous; and third, that the Soviet people has created everything by itself, without borrowing anything from without.

Unlike current practice in Western historical research, the Soviets try to prove that the Eastern Slavs did not come into the light of history relatively late, as historical newcomers, but are as old a civilised people as any other. Accordingly, Professor A. Udaltsov lays down that the predecessors of the Slavs may be traced back to the third millennium B.C., and that they owe their origin and the modifications to be found in their history not, as had been assumed, to migrations of particular races, but to their own inner development. (*Vopr. Ist.*, 1949, no. 2, pp. 14 *sqq.*, "The problem of the origin of the Slavs in the light of contemporary archaeology".)

The Scythians

Such is the explanation also of the special interest in the Scythians and Antes as the possible ancestors of the Slavs. The incorporation of the Scythians, who lived 2500 years ago in the steppes by the Black Sea, in the Soviet Union has four important advantages.

To begin with, it contributes to carrying Soviet history farther into antiquity. Secondly, it becomes possible with the help of the Scythians, thanks to their close association with the centres of ancient history to their west, to make both Persian and Greek history into a marginal contribution to Soviet history. This leads to the most extraordinary conclusions: according to Scythian legends the Scythians were descended from Heracles, who had himself sprung from the loins of Zeus. Thus the bow is stretched actually from Stalin's Kremlin to Zeus' Olympus. The third advantage was temporary, but played a part during the Second World War that should not be underestimated. Various characteristics of the Scythian strategy against Darius, the king of the Persians, were held up before the Russian army and people in 1941 and 1942, in the days of their defeats, as models to emulate. It was said (for instance, in an article by Professor A. Mishulin, *1st Journal*, 1943, nos. 8–9) that 2500 years ago the Soviet peoples (which in this case meant the Scythians) developed a particular strategy: they withdrew before the attack, deep into their country; under a "scorched earth" policy they left only ruins, with which the invader could do nothing, and they left behind them partisans to harass the enemy's advance and his lines of communication, until the enemy lines were so extended and thinned that a counter-attack could be made. Similar tactics, the political officers explained to the troops, were pursued by the Soviet peoples against Charles XII of Sweden and against Napoleon, and in the same way they could bring the war against Hitler to a victorious conclusion. Even that did not exhaust the possible uses of the Scythians to the Soviet ideologies. Professor Udaltsov showed that the Scythians were not a homogeneous people but a federation of several peoples. It followed that the Scythian fore-fathers of the Russians practised "friendship among the peoples", of which there was now so much talk in the Soviet Union; they were a sort of ancient Soviet Union; and when Professor Udaltsov came to the conclusion that they "formed a synthesis in their civilisation of West, East, and South", this too, was an attempt to show that these ancestors already had a "supra-national civilisation" such as the Bolsheviks were now adopting for the Russians.

The tribe of the Antes was dealt with by Professor P. N. Tretyakov in a fundamental work, "The Antes and the Rus' ", in the journal *Soviet Ethnography*.[1] He states that the Antes were largely responsible for the appear-ance of so high a civilisation so quickly in Kiev. The Antes were described by him as "the heirs of the millennial civilisation of the region north of the Black Sea"—not, for instance, of the Hellenes.

Anti-Norman

Pokrovsky had written of the origin of the first Russian States: "According to the traditions, the

[1] 1947, no. 4, pp. 71 *sqq.*, published in German in *Sovietwissenschaft*, 1948, no. 2.

founders of the first important States in the Russian plain were not Slavs but immigrant peoples—in the south, Khozars, who had come from Asia, and in the north the Varangians, who were natives of the present-day Sweden. Later the Varangians conquered the Khozars, and remained the sole rulers throughout European Russia. Recent pre-Soviet historians have challenged this version from patriotic motives: it wounded their national pride that the first rulers of the Russian Slavs were aliens. . . . This is of no more importance than the fact that the first princes of Novgorod and Kiev whose names we know were of Swedish origin (as is indisputable)."[1]

So lordly, not to say ironical, a treatment of Russian history is no longer possible today—far less possible than under the Tsars. Woe to the historian in the Soviet Union who fails to seize every conceivable opportunity to condemn outright "the Norman theory of the origin of Russian State life, which transplanted on Russian soil views of German nationalist historians". He commits himself just as seriously as if he claimed that capitalism is superior to Bolshevism. He can no longer venture even to mention the Norman theory as a conceivable hypothesis, any more than he could quote Trotsky or Tito. The classical story tells of the invitation sent to Norman chieftains by Slav tribes, in the famous sentence, recorded in a chronicle, "Our land is wide and wealthy, but there is no order therein; come ye, therefore, and rule over us." The chronicle also records that the Russians took over that name from a Norman tribe so called. But in Pankratova's *The past*

[1] *Geschichte Russlands*, Leipzig 1929, p. 21.

The New Doctrine

of the Soviet Land (German edition, Berlin 1947),
there is no mention at all of the Normans (or of the
Varangians), and the Varangian chieftain Rurik, who
founded the first Russian dynasty, is also left completely
unmentioned. Nor is any explanation of the word
"Russian" given. The Finnish scholar Valentine
Kiparsky brought evidence in a historical work that as
an inheritance from the Varangians (who in their
rowing boats had created a trade route between the
Baltic and the Black Sea) the rapids on the Russian
rivers had received Scandinavian names. After that he
was forced by pressure from Moscow to resign from his
position of director of the Finnish-Russian Institute in
Helsinki. At the end of September 1950 he had to
retire, after being bitterly attacked in the *Literaturnaya
Gazeta* of June 7th, 1950.

In *Russia's struggle to set up her State*[1] by the leading
historian of that epoch, B. D. Grekov, a work regarded
today as authoritative, we are put right on the subject.
We learn that when the Normans came to Novgorod
and Kiev those States stood already at a high level of
statehood and culture, so that the Rurikides only represented an episode in the middle of a long and great
history, and were certainly not the founders of Russia.

Now that the stain of the Norman theory has thus
been removed from Russian history, there is nothing any
longer to prevent the Soviet historians from presenting
the epoch of the Rurikides as a brilliant period not only
of Russian but of human history. Grekov writes on the
subject: "Only two States of the early Middle Ages

[1] Moscow 1945; German edition, Köhler und Amelang, Leipzig
1948.

played a decisive part in the historical destinies of Europe—the empire of Charlemagne in the West and that of the Rurik dynasty in the East." (p. 68.)

Anti-Thracian

Just as the Norman influence shrank to a transient and purely superficial episode, in order to prove the autochthonous character of Russian history, so layer after layer is removed from the record of the influence of Byzantium. Nothing at all that has ever happened on what today is Soviet soil can be allowed to trace its development authoritatively to foreign influences. Professor V. F. Gaidukevich published in a series of papers of the Soviet Academy of Sciences what is so far the most comprehensive and authoritative work (622 pp.) on *The Realm of the Bosporus (Bosporskoye Tsarstvo)*, in which he deals with the history of the south Russian steppe region around the Kuban, the lower Don, the Sea of Azov, and the Taman peninsula, in the period from the sixth century B.C. to the fourth century A.D. The book was at once subjected in the historical journal to sharp criticism. The writer, it was claimed, had greatly overestimated the Thracian—that is to say, a Western—influence on the development of that region; in reality it owed its advance to indigenous elements, primarily the Scythians, Sarmatians, etc. The cult of the river-god, it was contended, had not come from Thrace at all, but had been carried on from the earliest times among the races of that region. The dynasty of the Spartacids had not descended from a Thracian adventurer; on the contrary, it was indigenous, though there had been certain ties of relationship

40

with Thrace. For the rest, not only must the good elements have been autochthonous, but not even the bad could be admitted to have come from abroad. Every quality was autochthonous. Professor Gaidukevich was attacked for having attributed the fall of the empire of the Bosporus to the falling off of help from Rome. Even decay must not be attributed to foreign influences, however indirect. Gaidukevich ought, it was claimed, to have said that the decay had mainly been due to inner, not to external, causes.

Against the 'borrowers'

Instances of this sort may be drawn from the whole field of historiography. Whether it is a question of the time of Peter the Great or Catherine, the historians are required at all times to reduce to a minimum the "borrowings" from abroad. Those who do not sing this tune loud enough are accused of "cosmopolitanism, worthless kowtowing toward foreigners", virtually high treason. It will not even help them to try to ward off attacks by self-denunciation. Professor Rubinstein, for example, himself violently attacked one of his own works, *Russian Historiography* (Moscow 1941); in February 1948 he publicly attacked it, and, with many apologies, denounced himself for an "objective and academic view". In spite of this he has been attacked again and again down to this day in the semi-official press, as though he were not a repentant but a contumacious sinner. Concerning his *History of the Soviet Union until the Nineteenth Century*, published in 1948, we read:

"Professor N. L. Rubinstein proceeds here entirely

from the anti-Marxist, anti-scientific, idealistic theory of 'borrowing' as the basis of the origin and development of Russian civilisation. . . . He explains the level of civilisation of the Russian people in the period of the Kiev empire as due to the taking over of the heritage of antiquity and of mediaeval Byzantine civilisation. He attributes the advance of Russian civilisation in the twelfth century to Russia's extensive international relations, which made possible the penetration of world civilisation into Russia. Foreign influence, Rubinstein declares, determined the cultural development of the eighteenth century. Thus does countryless cosmopolitanism play with the culture of the great Russian people. Serious errors, originating in overestimates of foreign influences and depreciation of Russian culture and scholarship, are to be found also in the chapters on Russian cultural history in the *Textbook of the history of the Soviet Union*. The authors of these chapters frequently fall into the mistaken idea that various 'influences', 'borrowings', and 'repercussions' provided the basis for the formation of Russian culture. Especially in the chapter on the culture of the eighteenth century there are many errors. In the assessment of Russian statesmen the author continually lays emphasis on this or the other adoption of Western European theories and ideas and almost entirely forgets to give thought to the originality of our great men. Of Radistchev, for example, he says:

"'The literary form of his great work, *The Journey* [from St. Petersburg to Moscow], he owes to the English writer Sterne, the author of the *Sentimental Journey through France and Italy*. . . . Radistchev is a disciple of the French Rationalists and an enemy of mysticism, though in some of his philosophical works materialistic ideas are unexpectedly mixed with ideological conceptions which Radistchev acquired from Leibnitz while a student in Leipzig. His opinions on the family, marriage, and education come from Rousseau. General ideas on human freedom and equality were conveyed to him, as Radistchev himself states, by the French Enlightenment.'

"That is how the founder of the struggle for freedom against Tsarism and autocracy is characterised—the man on whom the Russian people look with pride, and whose work Lenin and Stalin so highly valued."[1]

Where a borrowing, however regrettable the fact, cannot be denied, the effort is made to minimise it, and to stress especially the modification made by the Russians in what they have borrowed: thus, for instance, Grekov says on the question of Christianity in the mediaeval history of Russia: "The capacity of the Russian people to build up their own civilisation and to modify what they take from other peoples is revealed in the destinies of the other Christian religions of Russia. . . . Very characteristic is the attitude of the Russian painters of ikons to the representation of Nicholas the Thaumaturge. That saint, of purely Greek origin, became in the Russian master's presentation in the frescoes of the Cathedral of St. Sophia at Kiev a typical old Russian, losing every trace of his original national character."[2] Thus does Grekov's book—very finely

---

[1] *Voprossy Istorii*, 1942, no. 2.
[2] *The Russian cults of the Kiev period*, German edition, Moscow 1947, pp. 56, 59.

produced and provided with impressive illustrations—
devote itself above all to proving the native quality of
Russian culture.

The struggle against borrowings is carried on with
such persistence that the Eurasian conception of Russian
history elaborated by *émigrés* is rejected by Moscow
although at the very time of energetic Asian expansion,
it would fall into line with Soviet ideas. The Russian
and the Soviet people are not to be allowed to be
subsumed in any more comprehensive conception, even
that of "Eurasia". The time is long past when Pokrovsky could write of the Slavs:

"Their language reveals the early Slavs to us as an
entirely primitive people. This is in full agreement
with the accounts that have come down to us from the
Greeks who observed the Slavs in that period of history
[the reference is to the sixth century A.D.] The Greeks
described the Slavs of that time as an entirely savage
people, dirty, half naked, even with no fixed dwellings,
living in tents, using poisoned arrows, and of great
cruelty. . . . When an upper class began to form among
the population in Russia, it found the old Slav religious
customs and practices and the magicians repulsive, and
began to introduce from Greece, together with silks and
gold ornaments, Greek priests and Greek customs."[1]

Grekov's most important and most comprehensive
work, *The peasants in Russia, from the earliest times down to
the seventeenth century*, the fruit of forty years of study,
was published in 1948 and awarded the Stalin Prize.
But the review sent out by Tass, the official news agency,
found nothing better to say than this: "In this work

[1] *Geschichte Russlands*, Leipzig 1929, pp. 20, 29.

Grekov has succeeded in destroying the old and completely false idea that Russia had limped after European history." (June 1st, 1948.)

Insistence on autochthonism implies not only stressing the positive rôle of the Soviet people and its forefathers, but the continual underlining of the negative part played by the world outside the Soviets. In the 1947 edition of the great Soviet Encyclopaedia, Professor I. Razgon wrote the article "Russia at the beginning of the twentieth century". In the *Historical Journal* he is reproached in all seriousness because from beginning to end of his article—he does not once make use of the phrase "Anglo-American warmongers" *Voprossy Istorii*, 1949, no. 6).

4. GEOGRAPHICAL PHILOSOPHY

One of the earliest cases of condemnation à la Rubinstein occurred in the field of the history of philosophy. In 1943 the Philosophical Institute of the Academy of Sciences of the U.S.S.R., published the third volume of an ambitious *History of Philosophy*, edited by leading Bolshevik ideologists (including M. Mitin and P. Yudin), dealing with the philosophy of the later eighteenth and the earlier nineteenth century, including the classical German philosophy. The three-volume work was soon awarded the Stalin Prize, and again, a little later, in the spring of 1944, the central journal of the party, *Bolshevik* (no. 7–8), issued a sentence of excommunication against the third volume for a false and dangerous interpretation of German philosophy. At the same time it was learnt that the committee that awards the Stalin Prizes had revised its decision and had retrospectively excluded the third volume from the award. It was now stated that the prize was awarded only to the first two volumes. In the succeeding weeks the *Bolshevik* article was reprinted in all the important Soviet journals, and everywhere in the U.S.S.R. it was made the central feature of the ideological teaching in lectures, press, and wireless. This article, we read, had drawn attention just in time to the danger of an intellectual dissolution of Bolshevism, and had brought the ideological adjustment of the Soviet man back to the right lines.

Two months passed between our reading of the *Bolshevik* article and the arrival of the third volume from Moscow. In those two months a whole flood of attacks against the third volume had swept across the Soviet Union, and when at last we had the volume in our hands we opened it almost with the feeling with which one digs up a mine. But where the violent attacks might have led one to expect the worst of heresies, we found nothing but a thorough and very tedious exposition of German philosophy, an exposition differing in no respect from what had hitherto been customary in Russian Marxist literature on the subject. In the case of Hegel, for instance, there was praise for everything in his works that fitted into the Marxist system, and condemnation of all that did not. Those who had knowledge only of volume 3 and of the *Bolshevik* article were faced with a complete enigma, hopelessly entangled in the mass of quotations from Hegel, Marx, and Lenin. Only when one placed this outbreak against volume 3

in the wider context of the ideological change in the
U.S.S.R. during the last decade, did one find the key to
it.

The authors of volume 3 described the development
of Western philosophy through the Enlightenment,
Rationalism, and classical German philosophy down to
Hegel, whose system was turned upside down by Marx
but still adopted by him; the classical German philosophy was thus presented as the forerunner of Marxism,
Leninism, and Stalinism. That treatment had been the
accepted rule in Soviet philosophical writings, but it
was so no longer. In the discussion of nineteenth-century
philosophy started by the *Bolshevik* article, therefore,
emphasis was laid on the demonstration that not Kant,
Schelling, Fichte, and Hegel, but quite other men were
the real giants of philosophy. "Our classical Russian
philosophy of the nineteenth century, represented by
Belinsky, Herzen, Chernyshevsky, and Dobrolyubov,
forms the peak of philosophical thought. . . . In its
development Russian materialistic philosophy was
independent of West European philosophical thought,
and often far ahead of it. In the realm of sociology
and politics the classical Russian philosophers were
thinkers no less independent and original than in the
field of logic and theory of cognition. . . . No philosophical revolution in the West can compare in importance and power with the ideological revolution that has
taken place in the consciousness of the Russian people,
thanks to the Bolshevik party and its leaders, Lenin and
Stalin."[1] "Chernyshevsky's chief merit is that he
exposed the mean and vulgar nature of Kant and

[1] *Bolshevik*, 1944, no. 12, pp. 11–27.

Hegel," declared a party orator at that time. (Radio Irkutsk, October 28th, 1944.)

Thus, the stages of modern philosophical advance are represented by Belinsky, Herzen, Chernyshevsky, Dobrolyubov, Marx, Lenin, and Stalin. In reality the four first-named were not philosophers at all in the true sense of the word; none of them worked out a philosophical system or regarded himself as a philosopher; they were writers, critics, publicists.

We may therefore say that the error of the authors of volume 3 did not lie in the realm of philosophy or even of political science, but in that of—geography. They committed the offence of describing the classical German philosophy as the summit of political thought in the pre-Marxian period and as an inseparable part of the intellectual development of mankind, whereas they ought to have depicted that development as in the main the achievement of men who belonged to "Soviet history".

So great is the unfortunate Soviet historians' and philosophers' fear of offending against the commandment about autochthonicity or native origin, that they are going to absurd lengths and tumbling over one another in their eagerness to respect it. M. Yovchuk, for instance, wrote in *Voprossy Filosofii* (1949, no. 3, p. 205) that Russian philosophers were the first to unite materialism with dialectics. This was too much even for *Pravda*. It solemnly laid down that "It is well known that that problem was solved by Marx and Engels." (*Pravda*, September 7th, 1949.) There is a limit to everything. Or, rather, there used to be. Since the *Pravda* article appeared, two years have passed. In that period the change in the Bolshevik view of Marx and Engels has become more marked. We shall return to it at the end of this essay.

From the new attitude to the people (see Stalin's toast to the Russians and his declaration at the Finnish reception, or Mavrodin's "The people are eternal") there was bound to come a new attitude to the language. That step has been taken in the many pamphlets and articles that appeared in the U.S.S.R. in the summer of 1950 on the subject of Soviet linguistics. Until a few months ago, Soviet philological research had been under the influence of Nikolai Yakovlevich Marr. Marr, the son of a Scotsman and a Georgian woman, was a striking man. I remember him especially among the many Soviet participants at a scientific congress in Berlin at the beginning of the thirties. In many ways he looked like the typical "professor" of the caricaturists of a few decades ago—rumpled hair, uncared-for clothing, stained lapels, in a word, a "genius". He was no longer at the height of his activity, but he had behind him decades of intensive philological study, particularly of Caucasian languages. Of lively rather than profound mentality, he had plunged into Marxism after the victory of the Revolution. He spent the rest of his life in the effort to make linguistics a Marxist science, and to squeeze language as well as he could into the Marxist historical process.

Complicated, indeed abstruse, as is the Marrist philological doctrine born of these efforts, its basic idea

49

is simple. Proceeding from the Marxian differentiation between the material basis and the ideological super-structure of human society, Marr assigned language, together with philosophy, religion, art, and so on, to the superstructure. He could do this with a clear conscience as the founders of Marxism had said nothing to the contrary; on this point they had said nothing at all. Since, according to Marx, the superstructure is some-thing secondary, borne, indeed produced, by the basis, the primary, Marr regarded language, including grammar, as a function of the economic and social conditions. Marx had described feudalism, for instance, as an epoch of human society through which all peoples had to pass, though at quite different times, an epoch through which all peoples pass in much the same way; Marr accordingly taught that the languages of peoples at the same stage of development had funda-mental similarities. Thus, although the Georgian and Armenian languages were of quite different philological origin, Marr contended that the Georgian feudal language and the Armenian feudal language were more closely related in system "than either of those languages is to the vernacular of its native country".

Marr had triumphant success with his theory. What he taught seemed to fit in excellently with the effort, visible in every field after the victory of the Revolution, to create "Marxist sciences". That was the time when the elements of the new supranational "language of Socialism" were making their appearance, artificially formed words like kolkhoz, Comintern, Comsomol, used by all the peoples of the Soviet Union. Those were the days when the Bolshevik leaders liked to hear Marr orate: "At this moment of revolutionary creativeness it is really comic to talk of reform of the Russian language or grammar. . . . There can be no question here of a reform but of a change of the norm of the language, a shifting of the language on to the new track of a real mass-language. What is needed is not a form or even a reform or a new decoration for an old content, but a fresh framework, with a new function, of new language material for the whole Soviet Union, the whole world."[1]

At his death in December 1934, Marr was the great philologist of the Soviet world. His influence even increased after his death. Until a very little while ago he was praised, not only in the U.S.S.R., but wherever the influence of Bolshevism reached, as the great authority in the field of philology. (For example, "The philological sciences of the Soviet Union. In memory of N. Y. Marr," *Tägliche Rundschau*, Berlin, December 15th, 1948, and the brochure by G. P. Serdyuchenko, *N. Y. Marr, the founder of Soviet materialist philology*, published in Moscow at the beginning of 1950 by the People's Ministry of Education.)

The Pravda *discussion*

For a number of reasons (we shall return to them; they were mainly the same as those that determined the liquidation of the historian Pokrovsky), Marr's linguistics were later found unsuited to the climate of Stalinism. Accordingly, the party executive decided to extirpate Marr's teaching and influence—fifteen and a half years after his death, when whole generations of

[1] *Selected Works*, vol. II, p. 375, quoted in *Bolshevik*, 1950, no. 15, p. 10.

philologists had been brought up in his spirit. It was further decided not to destroy Marr by a decree, but to do so through an—ostensibly—free discussion.

On May 9th, 1950, *Pravda* published an unusually long article, filling more than two whole pages, "On some questions of Soviet philology", by Professor A. S. Chikobova. The article was introduced by an editorial note to the effect that it was considered "essential to organise a free discussion in the pages of *Pravda*". After that, every Tuesday there was a special supplement to the paper, devoted exclusively to philological questions. This was very striking when it was borne in mind that normally, in order to save paper, *Pravda* has only four pages. The printing in *Pravda*, with its circulation of many millions, and then in many other newspapers and periodicals, and finally the publication of millions of brochures, represented a proceeding on an unusual scale, requiring the conversion of whole forests into paper and therefore a proceeding that must have a purpose going far beyond that of a purely learned philological discussion between scholars.

Stalin's five letters

The purpose became clear when on the seventh Tuesday, June 20th, something entirely unexpected happened: Stalin intervened—for the first time for eleven years in a question of ideology. He did this not in an article but in a letter—a letter, however, that covered a page and a half of close print. The following Tuesdays brought further contributions from various philologists. Then there appeared four further letters from Stalin, one on July 4th and three on August 2nd.

The New Doctrine

No gift of prophecy is needed to foresee that those five letters of Stalin's on linguistics will play in the publicity of the Soviet world, within and without the U.S.S.R., much the same part as the Epistles of Saint Paul to the Corinthians. Already they are described not as articles or letters but as "works" (*trudy*). They will play that part all the more since they deal not only with linguistic but with a number of other questions, three of which will be referred to later in this essay: the rôle of the State, Stalin's doctrine of the "superstructure", and the relativity of Marx.

A book might be devoted entirely to the five letters, dealing not only with their content but with their form. Just compare the openings of the letters and what those openings are intended to express (and do express for many Russians)—the benevolence of a father of his country, the condescending intimacy with the people, the sly modesty, the laconic brevity, the arch aloofness from the party bureaucracy. Let us quote:

(FIRST LETTER)

"I have been approached by a group of comrades of the young generation with the suggestion that I should state in the press my opinion on questions of philology, particularly in the section that concerns Marxism in philology. I am no philologist, and naturally I cannot satisfy the comrades. As for Marxism in philology and in other social sciences, with that question I am directly concerned. I have therefore agreed to give an answer to a number of the questions put by the comrades.

Stalin versus Marx

Comrade Krasheninnikova: I reply to your questions. "Your article shows convincingly . . ." [There follow a few lines giving Comrade Krasheninnikova's question.] Naturally language. . . .

Dear Comrade Sansheyev, I come very late to my reply to your letter because your letter was only yesterday passed to me by the staff of the C.C. [The Central Committee of the party].

To Comrade A. Kholopov. I have received your letter. I am a little late with my answer because of pressure of work."

Stalin's new doctrine

We confine ourselves here to the main ideas of Stalin's doctrine concerning language, which we may sum up in eight points.

1. Language does not belong to the superstructure—still less, of course, to the basis. It is something independent, and is therefore not conditioned, as Marr asserted, by the material and social substructure.

2. Language is not the affair of particular classes, but the affair of the whole people. ("Language was not created by any single class, but by the whole community, through the efforts of hundreds of generations.

54

. . . Consequently, it was also created as a single language of the whole nation, common to all members of the community. . . . The national languages are not class languages but languages of the people." First letter.)

3. Languages must not be confused with dialects or jargons. ("To suppose that dialects and jargons may develop into independent languages, which would be capable of driving out and taking the place of the national language, is to lose historical perspective and to abandon the positions of Marxism." First letter). (Words or expressions associated with particular classes "form scarcely one per cent of the total language material. Consequently the whole remaining overwhelming mass of words and expressions and their semantic (i.e. signification) are the same for all classes of society." Second letter.)

4. A language is not a matter of a historical period, but—measured by the duration of historical periods—eternal. ("A language is the product of a whole series of epochs. . . . Thus it lives incomparably longer than any particular substructure or superstructure." First letter.)

5. There are no ideas without language. (Second and fourth letters.)

6. When various national languages come together, they do not mix to form a new language, but one of them prevails over the others and establishes itself. (First letter.)

7. The Russian language, with which in the course of historical development the languages of a number of other people came into contact, came always out of the

55

rivalry as victor. Naturally the vocabulary of the Russian language was enlarged on these occasions, but this not only did not weaken the Russian language, but, on the contrary, enriched and strengthened it. (First letter. Nothing to do, no doubt, with "borrowing"!)

8. It is not stated, but it follows from points 6 and 7, that in the future, too, the Russian language, when it comes into contact with others, will emerge as victor.

1930 and 1950

This new doctrine of Stalin's has a snag for its author. Stalin had declared earlier (for instance, in 1930, in his speech at the sixteenth party congress) that "the national languages will flow together into a universal language, which, of course, will be neither Russian nor German, but something new". In his fifth letter Stalin goes into this contradiction. He solves the difficulty as follows: his linguistic theory enunciated in the five letters (our point 6) is valid for the time up to the victory of Socialism throughout the world; the view, on the other hand, formulated by him at the sixteenth party congress, and earlier, concerning the disappearance of national languages had reference to the time when Socialism of the Bolshevik type had won through all over the world. In this way Stalin's statements of 1930 and 1950 can in fact, on the surface, be reconciled. In reality, however, we have here an unmistakable advance in Stalin's views on language.

In any case, however, if we consider these views of Stalin's in 1930 and 1950 in the concrete, we get the following picture: until further notice, that is to say, until the worldwide victory of Socialism, Stalin's view in 1950, given by us in points 6 and 7, of the competition between languages and the continual victory of Russian, remains valid. Thus we have to assume that, until further notice, the Russian language will also continue victoriously to oust the other languages. Accordingly, at the moment of the "victory of Socialism on the world scale" the Russian language, through its immanent victoriousness, should already have gained such widespread predominance that in the process then starting of the formation of a world language it will have overwhelming influence.

If Stalin was serious in his ideas of 1930, then in the two decades that have followed he should have had an opportunity to prove it. In the past he had laid down that the development towards an international language would set in after the suppression of separate nationalities by others had ceased. (Relevant quotations from Stalin in V. Vinogradov's article in *Bolshevik*, 1950, no. 15.) Now, according to Moscow's daily reiterated assurances, the oppression of nationalities within the U.S.S.R came to its end at least thirty years ago. The fact that, according to the Bolshevik teaching, that oppression has by no means ceased in the world outside the Soviet Union, should not prevent the Union from setting a good example in its own territory with its dozens of nationalities. The better Stalin has proceeded with the achievement of Socialism, indeed Communism, within the U.S.S.R. (in spite of "capitalist encirclement"), the better he should have been able to proceed (in spite of "national oppression abroad") with the development of the supranational language within the U.S.S.R. If he had been serious about it. Obviously he was not in the least.

Stalin versus Marx

'Don Quixote of Linguistics'

To get an idea of the part played by Stalin's five letters today in the intellectual life of the U.S.S.R., it is enough to turn over the pages of any learned journal. We have in front of us the latest issue of *Voprossy Filosofii* (*Questions on Philosophy*), which appears three times in the year. In this issue, under the general heading "Scientific Life", is an article on "The Study of the New Works of J. V. Stalin". From it we learn that the scholars belonging to the Philosophical Institute of the Academy of Sciences of the U.S.S.R." have begun a "profound study of Stalin's new labours". To begin with, in the various departments of the Institute 35 professors gave addresses on the contribution to philosophy made by the Stalin letters. Then there were some plenary sessions of the Institute on the subject.

All the speakers, whose addresses are reproduced in summary, emphasise the extraordinary importance of the Stalin letters to philosophy, logic, psychology, the natural sciences, sociology, and every branch of science. (In an article in *Bolshevik*, 1950, no. 14, G. Alexandrov adds to that list "the historians, economists, jurists, and historian of literature".) At a meeting of the editorial staff of *Voprossy Filosofii* arranged at about the same time, one of the editors declared that henceforth the Stalin letters would govern the labours of his colleagues and himself in their philosophical and editorial work, and he expressed his sincere regret that space had been given to Marr's theories a little earlier in a journal.

Already a whole literature has come into existence on the Stalin letters. All writers throw scorn and reproaches on the man who but recently had been an unquestioned authority: now they call him the "Don Quixote of Linguistics". His "school" and "disciples" are referred to only in inverted commas—a death-sentence and worse. At the same time Stalin's doctrines are being explained to the population, literally in tens of thousands of meetings, all over the country.

The bond of union

What can have been the reasons that led Stalin and his advisers to proclaim this new doctrine, and to proclaim it at this moment? After all that we have said here about the development of the new historical picture of the world painted by Bolshevism, it will be intelligible that there is no longer any room in the Soviet Union for such a philological doctrine as Marr's. When a people, and especially a certain people, namely the people of Soviet Russia, is brought from the periphery of the current ideology very nearly to its centre, it is no longer possible to retain a linguistic theory in which the national languages, like the nations in Pokrovsky's works, are no longer credited with independent value and are treated as only impersonal, transitory stages of world history, now quickly approaching their end. The new philological doctrine thus sends out an additional appeal to the Russian and Soviet people, as a Chosen People, to make special contributions to the victory of Bolshevism in the world.

Further, in the same way as the magnifying of the nation the magnifying of the national language represents an attempt to combat the centrifugal elements in the new class formation. As the introduction of payment in proportion to work done (Stalin's speech of June 23rd,

1931) began to have effect in the creation of poor and rich, upper and lower, to an extent regarded earlier as impossible in a "Socialist country", the Soviet leaders found themselves faced more and more with the problem familiar to every government in countries with differentiated social classes, namely class antagonism. Hence the emphasis laid again and again on the fact that a language is a "universal national" asset, that it belongs to the whole nation and not to particular classes. The language is to be the bond of union between all citizens.

In his first letter, Stalin writes: "The cessation of all economic relations between the classes would mean that all production must come to an end. But the ending of all production leads to the downfall of society. Obviously no class can be prepared to expose itself to destruction. Consequently the class struggle, however bitter, cannot lead to social disintegration." It is true that Stalin writes that in the context of remarks about classes in the pre-Bolshevik epochs, but should he not have applied it just as much to the present day? All the more since he has declared often enough that today there are still classes in the Soviet Union, though they are not the same classes as in the past. This is virtually saying to the Russian worker, who has bitter feelings about the enormous privileges of the Soviet upper class: "You and the upper class depend on each other. You can't want to set yourself against it and so expose yourself to destruction!"

Into new depths

The emphasis on the intrinsic value and the endurance

of the national language is one of the most extreme and most interesting consequences of the new Bolshevik picture of history. In his rediscovery of Russian history, Stalin has penetrated into strata of human reality in which the Fathers of Marxism had no interest; in his new doctrines of language he is descending to a yet lower stratum.

The upholding of the national language implies the strongest insistence on the national tradition, for it is the language that unites us with the remotest past of our people, and embraces its traditions. The step from 1934 to 1950, the step from the discovery of Russian history to that of the Russian language, is the step from a stratum of the national to a yet lower stratum, that of language. This is pointed out especially by the reader in Slav Philology at Heidelberg, Dr. Johann Schröpfer, in an article, not yet published, on Soviet linguistics. He writes that at times when, in view of external or internal dangers, a people has been urged to work for unity, the appeal to the common language has been one of the weapons of the political and intellectual leaders. In Russia, too, this was the case in the past. When at the end of the eighties in the nineteenth century party strife threatened to bring a complete split in Russia and among those living in voluntary exile, Turgenev, in one of his prose poems, appealed to "the Russian language" as an anchor of hope and a creator of unity.

But it was not only the thought of the Russians that led Stalin to celebrate the Russian language in this way and to provide it with the prestige of victoriousness over all the languages that come into contact with it. Stalin has recognised that language is of enormous importance as an instrument in empire-building. Here again he is not the first. But his intellectual forefathers in this course were certainly not Marx and Engels—just think what they would have said about his five letters!—but such men as the Persian king Darius, the founders of the Roman Imperium, the leaders in British and French worldwide expansion, and the Chinese emperors.

The Cyrillic victory

It is not long since the Kremlin was doing everything to restore their national languages to the peoples of Russia that had been liberated by the Bolsheviks from the Russification policy of the Tsars, and indeed almost to proceed to violence in presenting peoples that were still very backward in their development with grammars and dictionaries of their own. Today the Russian language is being made more and more the national language by all possible means; not only that, but the Russian alphabet is being made the national script even for the languages of non-Slav peoples within the U.S.S.R.

Originally, especially in the fight against the influence of Islam and of the Arabic script, the Latin script was made obligatory for a number of Soviet languages. But look now at the communiqués published in the Moscow papers on the sessions of the Supreme Soviet, in the sixteen languages of the federal republics (for instance, in *Izvestia* of June 13th, 1950). Only in the case of the four Baltic republics (the Karelian, Latvian, Estonian, and Lithuanian Republics) is roman type still used. The Georgians and Armenians are permitted to use their old alphabets. (For how much longer?) All the other languages are made to use the Russian (Cyrillic) alphabet, including the Kazak, Kirghiz, Uzbek, Tadjik, Turkmen, and Azerbaidjan languages, and even that of the Moldavian Republic, which formerly belonged to Roumania and possesses an official language resembling Roumanian. Efforts are already being made to declare Karelian to be an idiom of the Russian language. With this "Cyrillisation" the Bolsheviks are proceeding much farther than the Russifying politicians of the Tsardom.

Empire languages

One is irresistibly reminded of an event that took place some 2500 years ago. The dynasty of the Achaemenides had at first shown tolerance, almost indifference, in regard to the languages of the peoples it had subjugated, until one day, at the beginning of 520 B.C., Darius I commanded that his proclamation to the peoples of his realm should be hewn in stone on the face of the sacred rock Bagistana (Behistun). For this he made use of the Persian language, for which he had had a new and simple alphabet elaborated. The inscription on the rock of Bagistana and the five Stalin letters on linguistics, different as the two pronouncements may be, were both instruments of the policy of men engaged in the building and consolidation of an empire.

Still more striking is the significance of Latin in the building of the Roman Empire. Is it so unlikely that Stalin can have heard how Latin, starting from small beginnings, gradually became the language of an empire, and how Roman thought and Roman rule spread and were consolidated in proportion as the

Etruscan, Umbrian, Ligurian, Gallic, and other languages succumbed to the predominance of Latin?

The Russian language is used as a first-class political instrument not only in the territory already dominated, but wherever the influence of Moscow extends. "Fifty thousand students have given in their names in the Prague region alone for courses in Russian, in order to learn the language of peace and freedom", wrote *Rude Pravo* not long ago in Prague. It is learned from Poland and Czechoslovakia that in those two countries far more than half a million people in all are taking courses in Russian. It is stated that the textbook of Russian grammar is the best seller in Prague, and that more than 350,000 copies have been sold. In this connexion the words of one of the most prominent political writers in Moscow, D. Zazlavsky, published at the beginning of 1949 in the *Literaturnaya Gazeta*, may be quoted:

"No one who does not know Russian and cannot read the works of the Russian intellect in the original can call himself a scholar in the full and true sense of the word. . . . It may be seen in the history of mankind how in the course of thousands of years the world languages succeed one another. Latin was the language of antiquity and of the early Middle Ages. French was the language of feudalism. English became the language of imperialism. And if we look into the future, we see the Russian language emerging as the world language of Socialism."

It is one of the piquant elements of world history that this glorification of Russian is being pursued by a man who until a few years ago spoke Russian with a foreign accent, and whose mother tongue is Georgian.

The New Doctrine

6. THE STATE REMAINS

Not only the conceptions of the people and of language but the conception of the State has been subjected by Stalin to thorough revision. Lenin—to say nothing of Engels—wrote in his fundamental work in this field, his *State and Revolution* (written in 1917), of an early disappearance of the State, but Stalin came to an entirely different view. His idea of the State is much closer to that of Hegel and Lassalle. We need only read what Stalin said in the last part of his speech to the 18th party congress (March 10th, 1939) about the State; he forecast for the State a very different future from the disappearance prophesied by his Marxist predecessors. At that time he still based his contention that even after the victory of the Revolution in Russia a strong State would be indispensable, simply on the consideration that owing to its hostile capitalist environment the new Socialist community needed a State organisation with striking power in order to hold its own against external enemies and against saboteurs within its frontiers. At that time Stalin still considered it necessary to make an obeisance to Lenin by stating that Lenin had planned a supplement to *State and Revolution*, "in which he would undoubtedly have expressed the intention, supported by the experience of the Soviet power in our country, to elaborate and further to develop the theory of the State".

Now Stalin has presented a most important new theme, developed in his letters on linguistics, although it has little to do with linguistics. It is the new theme of the "active role of the superstructure". (We shall return to this in the final section of this essay.) Stalin states that the superstructure does not merely play a secondary part, but represents "the most powerful active force". As he includes the State in the superstructure, the State is thus given an unsuspected additional importance. This idea of Stalin's, expressed in his first letter, seemed to him so important that he had a long article (unsigned and so indicated as coming from the highest source) published in the *Pravda* of October 5th, 1950, "On Basis and Superstructure". In its third section we read:

"After the victory of the Socialist revolution the rôle of the superstructure in the creation, strengthening, and development of the new basis grows enormously. . . . From this comes the special creative rôle of the new Socialist superstructure and in particular of the Socialist State, which represents the principal instrument in the creation of the economic basis of Socialism. . . . Now, in the period of the gradual transition from Socialism to Communism, there comes into view in full power and energy the rôle of the Soviet State as the chief instrument for the building up of Communism."

In a full commentary by G. Glezerman (*Bolshevik*, 1950, no. 18, pp. 52–5), this idea is further elaborated, and in particular the active rôle of the superstructure in the creative task of the State in the field of education of the Soviet people is exemplified. We read: "The tasks of Communist education make it necessary to raise all the means of ideological work to a higher level—propaganda, agitation, press, literature and art, the further development of science, the improvement of the activities of the schools and other educational institutions, and so on. The measures resolved on before the war by the party of Lenin and Stalin for the uplifting of the science of history, for the improvement of the teaching of history in the schools, for the strengthening of propagandist work, and the party's daily efforts for the development of literature, art, and science—all this served the fulfilment of the task laid down by Comrade Stalin of developing the ideological superstructure of the Socialist community."

In this way the doctrine of the "active superstructure" serves not only to anchor the State for an indefinite time, but to legitimise all that is done daily in the field of intellectual terrorism.

In this way the State receives, in addition to the protection of the Socialist community, a tremendous second task, as instrument—and, we may add, scourge —for the further development of Socialism. And "State" means, in concrete terms, the party. "The leading and guiding force in the planned development of social life", continues the *Pravda* article, "is the Communist party."

Two leaps

With this new doctrine, moreover, of the rôle of the State the logical foundation is laid for the ideological justification of a feature that is typical of every successful and ageing revolutionary, his conviction that now is the time to make an end of revolutions. Thus Stalin develops the theme of "revolution from above"—for a Marxist, a truly revolutionary doctrine! Proceeding from his categorical rejection of the idea of sudden upheavals (*vzruivy*, explosions) in a language (First letter), he continues: "In general we must point out to the comrades who so love sudden upheavals that the law of transition from an old to a new quality through the channel of a sudden upheaval is not only inapplicable to the history of the development of language, but is also not always applicable to other social phenomena, whether in the substructure or the superstructure."

This idea, too, only briefly indicated by Stalin, is further developed in a special article in *Bolshevik* (1951, no. 15, pp. 8–20). We give, to begin with, the line of thought of the writer of the article, B. Kedrov:

Stalin, writes Kedrov, dealt in three works with the laws of development, first in his brochure *Anarchism or Socialism?*, which appeared before the First World War, then in the chapter "On dialectical and historical Materialism" in the *History of the Bolshevik Party* (1939), and thirdly in the letters on linguistics. In the two first works Stalin had spoken of only two forms of development, evolution and revolution. Under evolution he understood a series of small and merely quantitative changes. (Example from nature: water gets hotter or colder degree by degree.) Revolution, on the other hand, means a qualitative change. (Example: out of water comes steam or ice; the water changes its quality.)

Unlike that, the letters on linguistics contain something decidedly new. The qualitative and therefore revolutionary change is now divided by Stalin into two different forms. Stalin prefers to talk no longer of revolutions, but of leaps (*skachky*). From these leaps there come, wrote Stalin (and Kedrov), two forms. One he calls "explosion" (*vzryv*), the other "gradual transition" (*postepenny perekhod*). The new doctrine, explained to the Soviet population by Stalin in a few sentences, but by Kedrov in twelve printed pages, is that qualitative changes must take place not only in the form of explosions (as, for instance, the transition from capitalism to Bolshevik Socialism through the revolutionary explosion of 1917), but also through a gradual development. As an example from nature it is pointed out that water can, either, through raising to a high degree of heat under appropriate pressure, be changed explosively into steam, or, even without heating, gradually evaporate in an open saucer. In both cases the change is qualitative, and therefore under the preceding terminology revolutionary, but the first change proceeds explosively, the second gradually.

Comparisons between the development of mankind and the boiling of water are, of course, idle confidence tricks. But let us admit that they are possible. What matters here is not that argument, but why this new doctrine was developed by Stalin and elaborated by his disciples at this precise moment. Let us see what Kedrov himself has to say.

"The difference between a leap in the form of an explosion and a leap that takes place gradually consists in the following. In the case of the explosion-like leap the quantitative changes have accumulated gradually beforehand within the old quality, until suddenly the qualitative change takes place; thus it is a case of a great leap composed of a large number of smaller jumps proceeding simultaneously. In the second sort of leap, the gradual transition, the quantitative changes do not accumulate, but effect each time a little jump, and these little jumps take place gradually one after another."

Thus, explosion and leap, we are told, must not be

taken as the same thing. The explosion is only one of the two possible forms of leaps. Not every jump, not every transition from an old to a new quality, must necessarily, under all circumstances, take place in the form of an explosion.

The question now arises, in what cases the leap takes place in the form of an explosion, and in what in the form of gradual transition. In the reply to this question the new doctrine approaches the core of the subject. Kedrov writes:

"How is an explosion caused in the transition from the old to the new quality? An explosion takes place when the coming into existence of the new is held up by obstacles which can only be removed by the simultaneous pressure of all the new forces. . . . Thus, whether a gradual transition is possible or an explosion is necessary, depends on whether obstacles stand in the way of the new or not. Thus (Bolshevik) Socialism could not come into existence without an explosion, without the destruction of the bourgeois machinery of state and of the bourgeoisie as a whole."

That thesis opens the way for the doctrine that since the victory of Bolshevism no further explosive changes can take place within its realm, since the new which developments are striving to attain, namely Communism, has no obstacles in its way that require to be removed by explosive means.

This, however, leaves the difficulty that certain developments even after 1916 (especially the collectivisation of agriculture) cannot with the best of good will be described as "gradual transition". Kedrov therefore draws a distinction between "antagonistic" and "non-antagonistic" conflicts. But that is merely playing with words. For on the next page of his article it at last becomes plain what all this is aiming at. What matters is not at all whether conflicts are antagonistic or not (what, anyhow, are non-antagonistic conflicts?), but simply and purely whether the changes (as in 1917) are enforced by a revolution from below or (as in the collectivisation) by a decree from above. This is stated in so many words:

"In order to recognise the form of a leap, it must be determined whether that leap is effected from above, that is on the initiative of the existing state authority— and with the support of the popular masses from below —or whether the leap is effected from below, that is to say against the existing state authority." Thus writes Kedrov, and he quotes from Stalin's first letter on linguistics as follows:

"The transition to the Socialist kolkhoz régime in the village was a revolution that removed the old bourgeois economic system in the village and created a new Socialist system. But this revolution did not take place through an explosion, that is to say not by means of a destruction of existing machinery of state, but by means of the gradual transition from the old bourgeois régime in the village to a new one. This was possible because it was a revolution from above."

This states quite plainly what is at issue, namely the question whether a revolution had come from below or from above. It is true that in the above quotation from Kedrov there is a shamefaced admission, between dashes, of the condition that the revolution from above must receive support from below from the popular masses. Anyone, however, who actually lived through the collectivisation which Stalin adduced in support of his thesis (or anyone who even knows of Sholokhov's *Virgin Soil Uprooted*), is well aware that what happened was nothing but a revolution provoked, planned, and ordered from above, which, apart from exceptions, found no support from below.

No more revolutions

But even a revolution from above like the collectivisation will no longer be needed in future, according to the official version. At the time there were still bourgeois elements in the countryside (thus there was an "antagonistic conflict"), the overcoming of which required an act of violence—although from above—accordingly, Stalin deliberately uses the term "revolution" for that process. Now, however, it is declared that in the Soviet Union there are only "non-antagonistic conflicts" left, whose settlement no longer requires revolutions.

Q.E.D. The transition from the existing "Socialism" to the "Communism" aspired to is a qualitative transition. According to the doctrine of Marxism, qualitative changes are only possible by way of a revolution.

Today, however, revolutions in the Soviet régime are utterly undesired. Accordingly, the very word "revolution" is no longer permitted. People must speak only of "leaps".

The "gradual transition" is introduced as one of the two forms of the leap. So we arrive in theory at the delightful picture of a development, which, thanks to wise guidance from above, is to produce a vast qualitative change, namely the passage from Bolshevik

Socialism to ideal Communism, entirely painlessly in the leaps of a gradual transition.

All this sounds quite pretty—provided that an entirely new special position is arranged for the Soviet machinery of state. Stalin's scribes identify him with a god who not only knows the end toward which mankind is developing, but also the roads along which it will reach it, and who is also resolved to lead mankind along those roads to that end. For those who regard this view as right, there is no escaping from the line of thought of Stalin and Kedrov. He is delivered over to the omniscience and omnipotence of the Politburo.

The lonely master

Anyone, however, who is of the opinion that the laws of development, some of which Marx accurately defined, did not lose their validity at the moment when Stalin came to power, but remained valid and continue so to this day, will arrive at a quite different conclusion. He will come to the conclusion that Stalin's machinery of State, no less than that of earlier autocrats, is a thing that through its ponderousness and rigidity is bound to produce conflicts and revolutionary movements within itself.

The empire of the Caesars and that of the Tsars lasted for centuries, until internal conflicts and external pressure produced explosive changes. But in our day events move much more quickly. The Bolsheviks have themselves done everything to wrest millions of people from the lethargy of centuries through the mass education they have organised, and to teach them to think, and there is a good deal—especially the attitude of the

73

émigrés—to indicate that the effete and rigid supreme leadership in the Kremlin, in its iron grip of power, represents precisely the obstacle to the development of the people that virtually demands the appearance of revolutionary elements.

Since the days of the great death-bringing "purge", that is to say for some thirteen years, the supreme leadership, the "Verkhushka", has scarcely changed, and in the thirteen years before that Stalin's struggle against his rivals did not so much change it as, through the perpetual "liquidations", reduce it. Today this "Verkhushka" is completely dominated by the inner-most circle round Stalin, to whom almost divine honours are accorded. That inner circle is isolated from the 200 millions of the Soviet State by a thousand guards and walls. Twenty years ago, and certainly thirty years ago, Stalin personally and intimately knew everyone in the country who held a key position, and had carried on political activities with them for decades. The great majority of those men were "liquidated" in the massacre of the nineteen-thirties. Now there is solitude round the 72-year-old man. What does he know now of the thoughts and feelings in the lower levels of the pyramid on whose unapproachable peak he is enthroned? What does he know of the party members who are less than fifty years old? Or, indeed, of those born since the revolution of 1917, who now form two-thirds of the party members?

Stalin, sun, moon, and stars

He knows, of course, what his secret police tell him about them. And what the police told him suggested to him the new doctrine of the two leaps. That is not a good sign. For if the Soviet ideologues find themselves compelled today to spread the doctrine that there will now be only gradual transitions directed from above, and that every thought of revolutionary developments is a revolt, indeed, a blasphemy against the eternal law of the world itself, this shows, more than all the so-called secret reports on oppositional movements in the U.S.S.R., that in the depths not only of the Russian people but also of the Bolshevik party, there is a revulsion against Stalin's course that is serious enough to induce the party to propagate with all emphasis the doctrine that within the realm of Bolshevism no further revolutions are needed or permitted.

Kedrov even takes the trouble to bring in the universe to Stalin's support. There is a reactionary doctrine, he writes, of foreign astronomers that our solar system came into existence through an enormous explosion. Soviet scientists, however, have been able to prove that the planetary system owed its origin to a gradual development. If sun, moon, and stars came gradually into existence, how much more—so runs the new doctrine—will Communism, under Stalin's wise leadership, be realised without explosives! "The deep-seated qualitative changes on the road to Communism will take place gradually, *on the basis of the strengthening of the present régime, and not on the basis of its destruction or of an explosion.*"

Does not that sound more like a formula of exorcism than a statement of fact?

Stalin versus Marx

In opposition to hero-worshipping historiography to the theory that history is man-made, to the writing of history round persons, Marx brought forward the economic and sociological, the materialist, view of history. In that view individuals are not much more than agents set to work by a development proceeding in accordance with its own laws. This view of history was very much in vogue in the Soviet Union at first, and also in the school of Pokrovsky. The fight against Pokrovsky was a fight also for the recognition of the rôle of personality in history. Among the charges made against Pokrovsky was precisely that of having degraded personality to the status of a marionette controlled by the economic process. Soon after his "demolition" there appeared the first biographies in which personality was brought once more into the foreground. The first of these was the novel about Peter the Great written by Alexei Tolstoy on his return from emigration, and some articles in ideological or specialist journals, re-examining the significance of personality. Other novels, films, and plays have dealt—no longer in hostility but in patriotic pride—with Alexander Nevsky, Ivan the Terrible, and such Tsarist generals as Kutusov. Then, in the last ten years, the Stalin cult became so important an element in the state and public life of the U.S.S.R. that no further evidence need be offered here to show that personality once more counts for something.

The New Doctrine

8. SLAVS OF ALL THE WORLD

For Marx and his disciples, the classes into which a community is divided were the important political reality. Nations played for them an entirely subordinate part, and Marxists concerned themselves with them only because nations were still much in the peoples' minds and had to be taken into account in any political planning. So it was that there came into existence that early nationalities policy of Stalin's, which he brought down to the formula that the culture of the peoples should be national in form and Socialist in content. The purpose of that policy was to fulfil certain desires of the minorities concerning the outward manifestations of their culture, not because these were regarded as important in themselves, but, by satisfying the peoples' expressed desires, to chain them the more effectively to Bolshevism.

While the nation was regarded as a regrettable evil and a relic of the past, race was entirely rejected as a political factor. Political movements based on race were sharply attacked, whether they were Nazi or pan-Slav. Shortly before the outbreak of war with Germany, pan-Slavism was officially branded as a "reactionary feature of Tsarism". But the war had lasted only a few weeks when there came an entire change. On August 10th, 1941, the first Slav Congress assembled in Moscow, soon to be followed by others. In June 1942 there appeared a new monthly journal, *Slavyane* ("Slavs"), with a cover decorated with ancient Slav devices. The arguments advanced in the articles in this periodical—so far as they were not devoted exclusively to whipping up the

77

fighting spirit—were strongly reminiscent of the nine-teenth-century pan-Slavs. A pan-Slav Pantheon was erected for such men as Hus, Kolar, Skobelyev, and all others who had been militants of Slavdom. And again and again there sounded the appeal to the "Slav brothers" of Poland, Czechoslovakia, Bulgaria, and Yugoslavia, to support the Soviet Union in its fight against the Germans.

After the war the slogan "Slavs of all the world, unite!" lost some of its importance. It is used now mainly in appeal to the Slavs living beyond the frontiers of the Slav States of eastern Europe, those of the forests by the Spree, in the Soviet zone of Germany, or the Slav communities in the United States. The pan-Slav tune is played much less frequently to the Slavs in the so-called People's Democracies than in the years 1941–5; otherwise they might hit on the idea that their membership of the Slav fraternity entitled them to special privileges.

9. THE RUSSIANS AS PACEMAKERS

It will now become intelligible that it is not out of any sentimental feeling for the late Zhdanov, or out of any nationalistic caprice, that a large part of the Soviet propaganda is devoted to demonstrating that it was the Russians who invented everything from the incandescent lamp and the aircraft to penicillin. The purpose is to prove that it is one of the characteristics of the Soviet people (as it was of its predecessors) to be ahead of other peoples in its development, or at least not to be hobbling after them. Grekov, for example, takes great pains to show that the assault of the Slav races on the Roman Empire did not come later than that of the Teutons. In this connexion he regards it as an element of the superiority of the Slavs to the Teutons that after making their historic contribution to the destruction of the Roman Empire "they set up their States on territory of their own, where every advance in the field of material civilisation was the fruit of their own achievement" (*Russia's Struggle*, p. 31), while the Teutons' civilisation was largely derived from the Roman Empire. A historian (in this case, once more the unfortunate Rubinstein) need only mention the works of the German cartographer Mercator to bring upon himself at once the reproachful question what he means by concealing the fact that in his work Mercator used Russian maps. (*Voprossy Istorii*, 1949, no. 6.)

10. THE IMPORTANCE OF PERIODISATION

This whole historiographical development in the U.S.S.R. finds its formal precipitate in the great part played by the question of "periodisation" (*periodizatsia*). In recent years and until quite lately, many conferences of historians have been devoted exclusively to this subject. From the conference reports we learn that the main concern has been first to extend the range of Soviet history to the earliest possible times (this we have already mentioned), and secondly—and this is more precisely the problem of periodisation—to begin each separate historical period in Russia as early as possible, and, if at all possible, earlier than among other peoples. The starting point of all these efforts is Karl Marx's doctrine that mankind passes through definite stages of development, the primitive community, the slave State, feudalism, capitalism, Socialism, and Communism. It is indisputable that it was the Russian people that, contrary to Marx's expectations, was the first to enter upon the stage of Marxian Socialism. If the Bolsheviks want to demonstrate that this was not a chance curiosity of world history, but that it had to be the Russians who would first achieve that step, then it had to be shown that the Russians (or their historical predecessors) were specially fitted by their whole nature to precede other peoples along the path predestined for mankind by the laws of the history of development.

According to the minutes of the session of the Historical Institute of the Academy of Sciences on December 13th, 1948, the whole session was devoted entirely to periodisation. (*Vopr. Ist.*, 1949, no. 4.)

Western textbooks assign the beginning of feudalism in western Europe to the eighth and ninth centuries, and in Russia to a later date, but Professor Bakhrushin set out to assign the beginning of feudalism among the Slavs of the sixth, seventh, and eighth centuries. At a session of the scientific consultative committee of the Historical Institute of the Academy of Sciences there was a heated discussion as to the use of the term "pre-feudal". Professor M. N. Tikhomirov definitely rejected that term. Pre-feudal, he said, meant non-feudal. Thus, instead of pre-feudal, the term "feudal" must be used. In this way the beginning of feudalism in Russia was pushed back a few more centuries. (*Vopr. Ist.*, 1948, no. 3, pp. 146 *sqq.*)

The New Doctrine

Competition for priority

Further: while Western historiography applies the term "enlightened absolutism" to the second half of the eighteenth century (Frederick the Great, Catherine the Great, Maria Theresa and Joseph II, Charles III of Spain), according to the minutes of that session of December 1848, enlightened absolutism began in Russia under Peter the Great, that is to say at the beginning of the eighteenth century. Competition has set in about the beginning of capitalism in Russia. Professor Druzhinin gave the year 1760, but before long (in an article in *Voprossy Istorii*, 1949, no. 6) he was beaten by nearly forty years by his colleague E. Zaozerskaya; in her article "On the question of the beginning of capitalist relations in the small manufactures of Russia in the eighteenth century", she set back the beginning of Russian capitalism to the twenties of that century.

The precedence in world history of the French Revolution is questioned by the insistence on two risings in Moscow, in 1648 and 1662, to which Western historians have devoted little attention; this is well over a century before the storming of the Bastille.[1]

In other sectors the matter is not so simple. Bolotnikov's rising has been promoted by Soviet publicity to a "Peasant War"; but it did not break out until 1606, a good seventy years after the Peasant War in Germany. The industry, however, of Soviet historians will certainly discover Russian peasant wars dating from the beginning of the sixteenth century. (Pankratova, p. 205, par. 47.) In the question, too, of the beginning of manufacture in Russia, at present assigned by the

[1] Pankratova, *History of the U.S.S.R.*, German edition, pp. 226, 248.

Soviet historians to the first half of the seventeenth century, precedence over western European development has not yet been established. (Pankratova, p. 223, par. 52.)

Thus, as we have seen, the question to periodisation is closely connected with the effort to establish priority. In one field, that of discovery, priority is actually the first concern. The claims to priority which the Soviets have put forward for discoveries in the region of the South Pole (with exceedingly practical political corollaries!), have been much commented on in the world press. Not so well known are the similar Muscovite efforts in the matter of the discovery of America. The historian, A. V. Yefimov, member of the Soviet Academy of Sciences, has been trying for years to antedate the discovery of Alaska by the Russians. He has now arrived tentatively with his hypotheses at the year 1649, thus winning for the Russians an advantage of more than a hundred years over past figures. He is now only 29 years short of the date on which the Pilgrim Fathers landed from the *Mayflower* on the east coast of America. Yefimov has also put forward the demand that the whole history of geographical discoveries on this earth should be critically examined, with a view not only to correcting it here and there but of fundamentally revising it in the spirit of Stalinism. He cannot sleep because of the worldwide admiration of the unique achievements of men like Vasco da Gama, Columbus, or Magellan, and so he sets alongside them as of equal moment the Russian penetration through Siberia and north and north-east Asia. "There were two great trends", he writes, "of colonisation. One led across the

Atlantic and round Africa to India, the other through Siberia to the Pacific." The discovery of America and of the sea route to India and China are assessed by Yefimov as amounting together to no more than the exploration of Siberia. The more actively the Soviet historians busy themselves with periodisation, the greater grows their ambition to break up the periods and for each sub-period to demonstrate Russian priority. Thus, for example, at the conference of historians in December 1947 a new term was brought into use by Professor S. V. Yushkov, namely "monarchy representing the orders", a sub-period of feudalism which he sets between the "early type of monarchy" and "absolute monarchy" and assigns to the latter half of the sixteenth and the first half of the seventeenth century. (*Soviet Science*, 1948, no. 3, p. 205.)

A gifted people

It is the special pride of the Soviet historians that a whole epoch of development is missing in the history of the U.S.S.R., that of the slave State. This enables them to prove that the Russian people (and its historical predecessors) has the characteristic not only of passing from one epoch into the next earlier than other peoples, but also of jumping past whole epochs, just as a child of genius, always ahead of his classmates, has no need to pass through one class or another. "In the field of ideas and politics our people is a whole epoch ahead of the peoples of other countries", writes the official journal of the Bolshevik party. (*Bolshevik*, April 1950, no. 8, p. 14.)

The comparison of human development in the Soviet

light with a child's schooling helps us to understand the Soviet historical doctrine. Both schooling and the progress of mankind are judged by the aim they are to attain. The aim of schooling is the fully developed human being, or, in terms of organisation, the graduate. The aim of human development is to the Marxist the paradise on earth, or, in terms of organisation, Socialism and Communism. Attendance in the third, fourth, fifth class of a school is not an independent objective, but is always valued by the degree to which it prepares the schoolboy for the final objective, the extent to which it brings him nearer to it; and similarly the various historical periods in the development of peoples are of no importance in themselves; they are merely preparatory stages on the road to Socialism, and the sooner they are passed through, if not entirely passed over, the better for all concerned. If we regard history from this angle, the whole perspective is altered. The conception of history is determined entirely from the final aim; it becomes teleological. Anyone who studies a period of history for its own sake may condemn an event which will appear commendable to the observer who assesses it teleologically. An excellent example of this is afforded by the judgment passed on Ivan the Terrible.

'Ivan Grozny'

In the past, in judging him by human and moral standards, historians condemned Ivan the Terrible. For Pokrovsky and his school, too, Ivan was the personification of evil, virtually a classic example and demonstration of the devilishness of Tsarism, a horrifying hypertrophy of the idea of monarchy. As recently as the beginning of the thirties I saw a film in Moscow dealing with Ivan's campaign against Kazan. It showed Ivan as the cruellest of conquerors, and the Tatars defending Kazan as heroic patriots. Since then the picture has entirely changed. A flood of books, films, and paintings have made a hero of the sanguinary Tsar, and the new historical doctrine applauds him as a progressive element—in foreign relations because he subjugated peoples that were at a lower stage of development than the Russia of those days, and at home because he prepared the way for the transition from feudalism to capitalism, and from the fragmented to the rigidly centralised State. It is very significant that one of the chief works on Ivan, that of Professor Wipper, appeared recently in a German translation under the title *Iwan Grosny*. The qualification "terrible", in use for centuries, was thus suppressed, and as it was difficult to find another appropriate German qualification the Russian term was used. But let nobody be surprised if the next edition is entitled "Ivan the Noble".

Pokrovsky was still free to call Ivan's mass murders mass murders, but Wipper's book appeared in Germany at a time when hundreds of thousands had already fallen victims to Stalin's "purges". It was thus desired to present Ivan's terrorist régime in such a way as to provide in advance a justification for Stalin's purges. Wipper accordingly objects to Ivan being "charged with merciless and often senseless atrocities", and adds: "Historical research in our day has convincingly proved the contrary: the facts adduced by Ivan's contemporaries explain the 'terror'" (Wipper's inverted commas) "of the period of crisis, 1568–72, and show that the perils that surrounded Ivan Grozny and his work were still more terrible, that the political atmosphere was even fuller of incipient treason than it had seemed to be to the earlier historians. Ivan Grozny must not be charged with excessive suspicion. On the contrary, his error lay in excessive trust in the Guards and the administration he had created, in lack of persistence in the struggle against the danger to him represented by the Conservative and reactionary Opposition." As an example of these perils (who can fail to be reminded of the grounds Stalin advanced for his purges?), Wipper mentions "a widely ramified conspiracy of the nobles of Moscow", who were so "unpatriotic and inimical to the State" that they planned an attempt on Ivan's life and schemed for the conquest of the Muscovite realm by the Sultan of Turkey. "Among almost all the persons in whose case research has been able to establish the reasons for their arrest, execution, or murder, the charge of high treason is typical." (p. 148.) Thus, as with Stalin, everything that elsewhere would be described and treated as opposition was punished as "high treason".

The claim of Russian leadership advanced by means of periodisation could be substantially reinforced if it could be shown not only that the Russians themselves advanced quickly from stage to stage and even entirely passed over some stages, but that they helped other peoples to make more rapid progress. Thus the idea of periodisation leads on to the next link in the train of thought here pursued by us.

The New Doctrine

11. THE MIDWIFE THEORY

Let us take Byzantium as an example. According to the new Soviet theory, Byzantine civilization was largely a Slav product. To prove this, Soviet historical research has been intensively devoted to the subject of Slav invasions of the Balkan peninsula and relations with Byzantium. After a mass of material on that question had been accumulated, sorted out, and published, Professor V. I. Picheta summed up the results in a work from which we take the following line of reasoning. (1) The Slav assault on the Balkan peninsula led to the collapse of the slave-holding structure of the eastern Roman Empire. The form of community which the Slavs brought with them provided the conditions for the Byzantine transition to the feudal economic system. (2) The characteristic Byzantine civilisation that now came into existence was a synthesis of the ancient civilisation with the independent Slav culture. (3) The Slavs brought about the rejuvenation of the eastern Roman Empire and the prolongation of its existence by a thousand years; they thus had a "progressive significance" for the eastern Roman Empire.[1]

This does not show priority of the Slavs over the Teutons; indeed, Picheta finds that the Teutons played the same part in relation to the western Roman Empire as the Slavs in relation to the eastern. Though, however,

[1] *See* V. I. Picheta, "Slav-Byzantine relations in the sixth and seventh centuries in the light of the Soviet historians", *Vestnik Drevnei Istorii*, 1947, no. 3, pp. 95 *sqq*; A. P. Mishulin, "The ancient Slavs and the downfall of the eastern Roman Empire", *Vestnik Drevnei Istorii*, 1939, no. 1, p. 307.

priority cannot be established (or at all events not yet), the superiority of the Slavs over the Teutons may be observed in another field. While in western Europe the fallen Roman Empire established its culture among the conquering Teutons (Roman Law, the Latin tongue, Roman municipal organisation, the Roman art of war), conditions in eastern Europe developed differently. "The new peoples, and particularly the Slavs, were able to utilise a number of military and technical customs of the ancient world, but in constitutional and ecclesiastical matters they were able to preserve their individual character."[1]

Progressive barbarians

For the rest, it will probably not be long before priority in time in the matter of the destruction of the ancient world is established for the peoples of the U.S.S.R. Grekov already points out that a decree of Protogenes, dating from the third century B.C., clearly shows that at that time "the Greek colony of Olbia passed through a very severe internal crisis accompanied by a successful assault by the barbarians surrounding it". It also appears from the decree that the attack on Olbia was carried out by Scythians in conjunction with the slaves of Olbia. (Grekov p. 20.)

Grekov proceeds to show that as a result of such attacks slave-holding communities introduced a new social order. This process continued gradually on an ever-expanding scale. At times Grekov's description of these events assumes a tone that gives rise to a suspicion that this Soviet author is trying to combat

[1] Grekov, *Der Kampf Russlands*, p. 31.

88

certain inferiority complexes in regard to the West that exist in the Russia of today, as they did in the Russia of past centuries, whenever the Russians notice, or imagine, that the West is looking upon them as barbarians.

The inferiority complex in general is an inexhaustible theme in Russian history. Perhaps it is most intimately bound up with the nature of the "authoritarian man". How can it be explained that the Soviet citizen, at a time when his country has reached the highest peak of power, becoming one of the two remaining world powers, shows more touchiness about everything and lives in perpetual suspicion of being denied full recognition, being set in the background, being "done"? That is the only possible explanation of the triumph with which Grekov places it on record that the inhabitants of Olbia, "Hellenes by birth, who kept up the custom of learning the Iliad and Odyssey by heart", followed not only in their social order but in their clothing the example of the "Scythian barbarians".

"It was much the same everywhere", writes Grekov, "where the two worlds met, one decaying and doomed, the other robust and looking into the future with justified hope, and showing itself able to breathe new life into the old and dying society. Evidently the past system of slavery could no longer be maintained . . . and the oppressed classes, including the lowest among them, the slaves, who had to live like animals, gave expression to their aspiration for freedom and for the ending of their oppression in planned mass revolts. At the same time young peoples rose to protect themselves from the systematic blood-letting which the slaveowners, hunting for the new manpower they so bitterly needed to apply to them. The young peoples sought also to set free both the actual slaves and the so-called free citizens, who were themselves oppressed by the slaveowners, and who, in the words of a Roman, had had enough of living under Roman laws. Those peoples, with the support of the popular masses of the slaveowning world, carried on the fight for their statehood with the aim of bringing down the old society and introducing new and, beyond doubt, more progressive forms of existence. . . . The Byzantine historian Procopius (6th century) reports in his *Secret history of the time af the emperor Justinian* as follows: 'The people went over in masses to the barbarians . . . they acted as if their homeland had been conquered by the enemy.' By 'barbarians' Procopius meant the Slavs." (pp. 19–26. The sentence quoted from Procopius implies that the people went over to the barbarians because they so hated their own upper class that they regarded it as an enemy that had conquered them).

Substitute "Soviet people" for "barbarians" and "Slavs", and "proletarians" for "slaves", and those sentences might have come from a propaganda speech in the Cominform in 1950 instead of a history of the early centuries of our era. At that time the Scythian barbarians were fighting against the highly civilised Western community of Olbia not in a war of conquest but as friends and liberators of the oppressed classes of Olbia, who for their part wanted nothing better than to join the barbarians, who represented the next higher stage in social progress. Today—so the propaganda would run—Soviets· and People's Democracies are pursuing the cold war against the decadent West simply in order to liberate its peoples and raise them to the highest level of human development, Socialism and Communism.

Kazaks uplifted

Favourite examples with which to compare this Soviet midwifery are drawn from the various phases of Russian eastward expansion. Here the contrast between the latest Soviet historical doctrine and that of Pokrovsky's time is particularly clear. Pokrovsky and his school drew a dark and repellent picture of the methods of Russian expansion into Asia. They had no need to exaggerate; the features of the expansion were really repellent, though no more so than those of the early Spanish colonisation in America. The works of the Soviet historians in the first fifteen years after the Revolution are packed with documents showing the atrocities of the colonisation of Siberia and other regions of Asia by subjects of the Tsars. The Soviet historians of today, however, in judging a historical process, are not concerned about whether it was sanguinary, treacherous, and brutal, but only about the relative stages of human development reached by the conquerors and the conquered. In the sixteenth century, when Russian eastward expansion began, Muscovy was a fairly progressive feudal State (a monarchy resting on the orders, as we saw), while the peoples of the lower Volga and in Siberia against whom the Russian assault was first directed were at the stage of early feudalism, and, indeed, in some cases were slave-owning or even primitive communities. Later, when expansion in central Asia began, the Russians had advanced a stage; they were at the outset of capitalism and their adversaries at latest in the final stages of feudalism.

The subjugation of those peoples by the Russians thus led to their being raised to a higher stage of development than that at which they stood at the time of their conquest. However cruel, therefore, may have been the methods of the Russian conquest, they were a benefit to the conquered—even if they did not know it or would not see it—as their development toward the Socialist paradise was accelerated.

The case of the Kazaks shows the political potentialities of this historical doctrine. The Kazaks (not to be confused with the Cossacks) are an Asian people living in the vast steppes north-east of the Caspian. On the subjugation of the Kazaks—a particularly gloomy and sanguinary page in the book of Russian history— the historian (Mme) Pankratova writes: "The inclusion of Kazakstan in Russia's sphere of influence had a progressive influence on the further development of Kazakstan, since Russia had then entered the path of capitalist development." (*Istoricheskyi Journal*, 1943, no. 11–12, pp. 86–87.) Here we see fully developed dialectical materialism. The destruction of the basis of the existence of a whole people, numbering many millions, with the annihilation of an upper class, is converted by the magic wand of dialectics into a blessing for the people.

Kirghiz helped on

Or another example, that of the Kirghiz. In an

article "On the union of the northern Kirghiz with Russia", A. Khassanov writes in *Voprossy Istorii* (1950, no. 7, p. 130); "In spite of the negative sides of the policy of colonisation of Russian Tsarism, the entry of the Kirghiz into the Russian Federation represented an advance. The Kirghiz people were faced with the dilemma between either remaining under the rule of Kokand or submitting to their northern neighbour, Russia. Objectively regarded, from the point of view of social development, the union of Kirghisia with Russia was a step forward. . . . The Russian State stood at that time higher in every respect than Kokand or any other Asian State. . . . The most positive element in the union of Kirghisia with Russia was especially the rapprochement between the Kirghiz and Russian peoples and the unfluence of the civilisation of the Russian people on that of the Kirghiz. . . . The Russian revolutionary movement began to give aid to the Kirghiz in their struggle against the exploiting classes. With the assistance of the great Russian people, the Kirghiz people passed by capitalism and entered into Socialism."

Even Christianity, which for so long was so despised by the Bolsheviks, is brought into this system of ideological instruments. It legalises, so to speak, the subjection of pagan non-Russian peoples by the Orthodox Russians, since at certain periods and under certain circumstances, for instance, through its rejection of slavery, Christianity served progress.

The Soviet historians have already reached the point at which they can scarcely conceive any longer any development of Asian peoples without union with

Russia and the progressive influence of the Russians. The historian B. G. Gafurov, author of the *History of the Tadjik people* (1949), is sharply attacked by the reviewers in *Voprossy Istorii* for his statement, entirely unintelligible to the reviewers, "that capitalism" (which in this case is regarded as a progressive force in comparison with the feudalism that had existed there) "would have developed in central Asia even without union with Russia, and perhaps even more quickly than under the conditions provided by Russian colonisation". (p. 390; *Voprossy Istorii*, 1950, no. 7, p. 164.) So the Tadjiks were not to be allowed even to have developed the evil capitalism unaided; even that had to be treated as brought to them by the Russians.

2000 years ago

It is the duty of the Soviet historian to show that the Russians played this rôle of promoters of progress everywhere and at all times. Thus, Professor A. Mishulin has established that in the first century B.C., in the Crimea, which was then a part of the Roman Empire, there was a revolt of Scythian slaves. "Scythian tribes, of Slav race, prepared here in the east a mighty blow against the dying and slaveowning civilisation of the Roman Empire", writes Professor Mishulin, suggesting the conclusion that two thousand years ago the Soviet people, in its Scythian incarnation of that time, played the part of liberator of peoples.

That theory leads to a very important conclusion, namely that all peoples which in the past or present have come into "Russia's sphere of influence" have thus been dragged in a motherly though painful embrace into the completion of their development in Socialism and Communism. Should a people have the stupid desire to liberate itself from that embrace, it would be a crime against the laws of evolution; it would then be necessary to take strong measures to rid it of such desires, just as a naughty child cannot be permitted to take a drink from a bottle of hydrochloric acid. The chief importance of this grandiose theory does not at all lie in the justification of Russia's past, but in the justification of the Bolshevik future. The theory already contained the ideological justification for bringing all other peoples and countries into the Soviet sphere. Whether it is a matter in the past of Poles and Bulgarians, in the present of Chinese and Koreans, or in the future of Persians or Swedes, since as yet only one people, the Soviet people, has climbed to this stage of Socialism and Communism, every other people chosen for uplifting the Soviet people must be full of deep gratitude to that people.

All the more annoying was it that in the U.S.S.R., in spite of rigid organisation of all the intellectual workers, it took years for the Soviet historians fully to understand the new general line. As recently as in 1945, for instance, there appeared two books on Kirghiz history, in which there were echoes of Pokrovsky's time; they were duly treated with harsh criticism. Thus, the *Literaturnaya Gazeta* wrote on December 7th, 1947, in regard to S. Abramson's "Sketch of the civilisation of the Kirghiz people", in tones of correction, that it is contrary to historical truth to say that the Kirghiz people was brought under Russian rule against its will. "In uniting with Russia, the Kirghiz people came closer to the

95

revolutionary representatives of the Russian people just at a time when the most revolutionary proletariat of all, the Russian, came upon the stage of history." At the same time the producers of the "Essays on Kirghiz literature" were rapped over the knuckles for describing the union of Kirghisia with Russia as "conquest". "Do not the author and editor know that as a result of the union (and not 'conquest') the Kirghiz people escaped from the danger of being enslaved by other States of the east, which were far more backward than Russia?" In an article in *Voprossy Istorii* (1949, no. 11, pp. 3 *sqq.*) it is stated that one of the chief tasks of Soviet historians should be to describe the age-old friendship between the Russian people and the other countries of the Soviet fatherland, together with the progressive historical rôle of the Russian people as uniter of peoples. (*Vopr. Ist.*, 1949, no. 11, pp. 3 *sqq.*) Once the Tsars were called the "Patron of the Russian soil"; today the Russian people has been promoted to the status of "uniter of peoples".

The adjustment of the history of mankind to Soviet Russian history has a further important advantage. If we look upon history as Pokrovsky did, without the centre now formed by Russia, many historical events are withdrawn from purely dialectical explanation. A French writer, Jules Monnerot, states in the Berlin *Monat* (June 1950) that "It was no part of the dialectics of the Inca civilisation to be extirpated by Catholic Spain": nor, he might have added, was it any part of the dialectics of Kirghiz civilisation to be destroyed by the Russian colonisers. From the standpoint of the classic dialectics of Marx and Pokrovsky that is entirely logical, but here Soviet historiography jumps into the breach and says that it is entirely in accordance with the dialectics of Kirghiz civilisation that it should be destroyed and converted by the salvation-bringing Russian colonisers, as a stage on the road to Socialism. And when Monnerot adds that it is not in the dialectics of Europe to be Bolshevised from the east, and so to receive, on top of its sound European "substructure", an alien, Bolshevik, ideological "superstructure", a superstructure, that is, which is conditioned by an alien, namely the Russian, substructure, the new Soviet historiographers have an answer to that too. They say: no matter about dialectics or superstructures or substructures; it is just the duty of the peoples of this earth to let themselves be raised from stage to stage by the Russians.

The historical labyrinth

It is understandable that the Soviet historians do not find it too easy to make their way through this complicated dialectical labyrinth. Sometimes, too, in their zealous and gallant compliance with the directives they shoot beyond the mark; for how can they know into what traps an excess of zeal may lead them? The historian M. H. Tikhomirov, whose task it was to write a work on the Turkish wars of Catherine the Great, described them with honest pains as wars of liberation. But instead of being praised as a patriotic Soviet historian, as he must certainly have expected, he found himself hauled over the coals in his specialist organ, *Voprossy Istorii*, and told that these wars of Catherine's "were of aggressive nature, although their

97

results, objectively regarded, were of progressive importance for Russia". (*Vopr. Ist.*, 1949, no. 11, pp. 3 *sqq.*) No wonder the poor Soviet historians scarcely know what themes they can turn to without getting chastised. For a time Oriental and Asian history was regarded as a relatively harmless field, "far from the shooting". But even this has now been doubtful for years, unless, indeed, one crept into the remotest hiding-places of the narrowest specialism. What this has meant is described in a leading article in *Voprossy Istorii* (1949, no. 4, pp. 3 *sqq.*), complaining of the scarcity of Soviet books and articles on the East:

"In recent years only a single Stalin Prize has been awarded for historical works on the East. . . . Many works of Soviet orientalists in the field of history have been subordinated to narrow philological interests and have a one-sided character. . . . With the exception of the first volume, published in 1940 of the *New history of the colonial and dependent peoples* . . . there has up to now been no textbook in the U.S.S.R. about the history of the East . . . and no comprehensive work on the history of China, Iran, India, Korea, Mongolia, and other countries of the East . . . In the fifth volume of *Sovyetskoye Vostokovedenye* (1948) we find in the section History ten articles, of which two are devoted to ancient times, three to the third to the sixth centuries, two to the fourteenth, two to the eighteenth, and one to events in the middle of the nineteenth century. Thus no one has come as far as the twentieth century." The reasons are obvious.

The same is true of almost every field. After the war the Soviet historians set forth a grandiose programme for a historiographical five-year plan. It included a comprehensive History of the U.S.S.R. in twelve volumes, a six-volume compilation on the history of the Russian towns, comprehensive works on the history of the Russian peasantry in the seventeenth and eighteenth centuries, and works on the history of the Russian proletariat, the Russian market, and Russian Balkan policy, and on Russian military history. Of this long list next to nothing has been completed. That is easy to understand. The Soviet historian may succeed in treating of subjects in the remote past or of narrowly specialist interest without danger to life or limb, but the last hundred years, and any wide historical surveys, are dynamite, which he shuns. The Academy of Sciences published a collection of historical articles to celebrate the thirtieth anniversary of the Bolshevik Revolution. The volume contained not a single contribution on the history of the Soviet régime; what it did contain was an article on southern Mesopotamia under the third dynasty of Ur, in the third millennium B.C.

The readiness of Soviet historians to take risks is not exactly increased when they cannot even rely on the guiding lines offered in their central journal, *Voprossy Istorii*, and learn, for instance, in no. 2 of the 1949 volume that the first number of that volume was behind the times, liberal, rotten, unbolshevistic, random, not serious, antiquated, cowardly, uncritical—in a word, wretched.

Polish falsifiers

For the rest, the Soviet historians are not the only persons whose profession has become full of risks. The same is true of foreign historians in so far as they are Communists or live in the States of eastern Europe that belong to the Soviet world, or in the Soviet Zone of Germany. A year ago, for example, in November 1949, the Czech historians had to arrange a conference in Prague devoted to "the fight against the influence of the Pokrovsky school on Czech historical research". It is highly instructive to read the way the Polish authors of the historical textbooks that appeared in Poland in 1947 were dealt with in *Voprossy Istorii* (1949, no. 4, pp. 99 *sqq.*). Particularly interesting is the way this official organ of Soviet historiography expressed itself in regard to the conflicts between the Soviet Russian and the national Polish writing of history. We find this, for instance: "Unfortunately these schoolbooks have found room for many statements derived from the spirit of a Polish Great-Power chauvinism. . . . The authors have unmistakably falsified history: in their description of the Battle of Grünwald [that is to say, Tannenberg] of 1410 they say nothing about the heroic behaviour of the Russian regiments, who stood firm in the battle to their death; they even write of the disorderly retreat of the Russians, which did not take place in reality. . . . They say nothing about the many wars fought by Lithuania and Poland against the State of Muscovy between the fourteenth and the seventeenth century being unjust wars. . . . They omit the fact that in 1654 the Ukranian people unanimously expressed the desire to be united with the Russian people—not with the Polish. . . . They have not the courage to admit that the union of the Ukranian and White Russian peoples with the Russian people, objectively regarded, was a progressive event, irrespective of the predatory character of the policy of the Tsaritsa Catherine II."

That summer there took place at Sofia a session of the Bulgarian Archaeological Institute. At that session it was discovered that Bulgaria had to create a new "Socialist archaeology" on the Soviet model. In particular, "every source of nationalism in archaeological literature must be cut off", and every national impulse that might show itself in the future in Bulgarian archaeology or historical research must be ruthlessly attacked. Everything that did not plainly and unconditionally incorporate Bulgarian history in Stalin's new historical system was to be accounted as "Bulgarian nationalism". The Bulgarian archaeologists were not spared from violent reproaches because so far they had failed to give the Bulgarian people "information based on serious and profound studies of the important expeditions and archaeological excavations in the Soviet Union, which had produced a real revolution in archaeological research". (*Neue Zürcher Zeitung*, June 26th, 1950.)

Conflicts of this sort will inevitably grow more frequent in proportion as Moscow forces into its new category of history the non-Russian peoples, and still more the peoples outside the Soviet Union, until the last Bulgarian and Polish historian has been made to fall into line—or Stalinism has disappeared from the world stage.

Three dilemmas

The result of all this for the Soviet historians is a

whole series of dilemmas, between the emphasis, for instance, on the requirements of periodisation and those of midwifery. Periodisation calls for the dating of the Slav invasion of the Balkans as early as possible. The theory of the midwife's rôle, on the other hand, requires that the Slav invasion should more or less fall into the period of the downfall of the slave-owning society of the Byzantine empire, for only in that case can it be contended that it was the appearance of the Slavs that brought the end of the slaveowning society. If the Balkans had been settled by Slavs before the sixth century, "the Slavs would not have solved any of the social problems in the destiny of the eastern Roman Empire", writes Picheta (p. 126). As, however, the Slavs cannot possibly do anything else but solve the social problems of other peoples, they must have migrated into the Balkans after the sixth century.

A further dilemma: the whole of the Soviet propaganda among the ancient peoples is built up on the contention that the national struggles of the peoples for liberation from their colonisers are good and progressive. How can this be reconciled with the other contention, that the struggle of the Russians against national liberators (as in the case of the Tatars or the Kazaks) is also good and progressive? That dilemma was quickly disposed of by "dialectical" phrases such as this: "The historically progressive character of the union of Kazakstan with Russia does not prevent the national struggle of the Kazaks for liberation, directed against the colonising policy of the Tsardom, from having been progressive." (*Vopr. Ist*, 1950, no. 8, p. 127.)

A third dilemma: the Russians have fought wars in the past not only against peoples that were one or more stages behind them in development, but also with peoples of the same stage or a higher one. It should then, of course, have been really a blessing for the Russians to be conquered by the peoples of the higher stage of development. But there is an answer to this as well. Since the Russian people is by nature the liberating people *par excellence* in world history, the people to whom it was to be given to be the first to climb up before all others to Socialism, its wars, even when carried on against opponents at a higher stage of social development, were always noble wars of defence, necessary not only on narrow patriotic grounds but in the interest of mankind. For from what has been said already the following point follows.

12. THE INTEREST OF THE SOVIET PEOPLE IS THE INTEREST OF MANKIND

The argument of the whole set of considerations here summarised is that everything that serves the progress of the Soviet people serves the welfare of mankind. This argument is advanced not only indirectly by the process of reasoning of the Soviet historians, but directly in so many words.

"The programme of the Communist party of the Soviet Union, the aims of our constructive work and the principles of Soviet state policy, are identical with the general direction of the historical development of the human race. . . . The rightly understood interests of all the progressive elements in the whole world are identical with the interests of Soviet policy. . . . In our age, since all roads lead to Communism, all those who take the part of the Soviet Union are historically in the right. All those who are against the Soviet Union are historically in the wrong. They are trying to stop the wheel of history. But that is impossible, and he who attempts it is broken and crushed by the course of history. . . . Every victory of our Soviet fatherland is a victory for peace and progress." (Khvostov, "Stalin's foreign policy". *Vopr. Ist*, 1950, no. 1. p. 38.)

Thus, for Soviet historians it is a definite duty "to give a full revelation of the importance of the progressive Russian civilisation for the development of the civilisation of other peoples." (*Vopr. Ist*, 1949, no. 11, pp. 3 *sqq*.) There can hardly be a worse offence for a Soviet historian than the neglect of that requirement.

"The countryless cosmopolitans of our day belittle the leading part played by the Russian proletariat. . . for the whole world. . . . They falsify and distort the world-historic rôle of the Russian people in the creation of the Socialist society and in the victory over the enemy of mankind—German Fascism." (*Vopr. Ist*, 1949, no. 2, "Tasks of the Soviet historians".)

Here it also becomes plain why Soviet publicity so monotonously repeats the declaration that the Soviet Union alone won the war against Hitler. The purpose here is not only to gratify the normal national pride, but to prove the uniqueness of the Soviet people and its heroic fight for the interests of mankind.

The special, leading position, moreover, of the Soviet people in the fight against Hitler is only a further "new proof" of the continually repeated assertion of the protective and liberated mission of the Russians on behalf of human civilisation, formulated, for instance, by Grekov with reference to the Russian part in the fighting against Mongol assaults: "No people in all the world had to go through so much, to make such sacrifices for itself and for others, as the Russian people. . . . Under the heavy hand of the Mongol nomads and semi-nomads, many civilisations came to their end. Only a small part of Western Europe remained unscathed until the Russian people had placed itself protectively before it." (*The Russian civilisation of the Kiev period*, pp. 109 *sqq.*)

Here, finally, it becomes clear why Tito had to be declared Public Enemy no. 1, of the Soviet Union. He had committed the primal sin of objecting to the principle of the absolute leadership of the Soviet Union. The only attitude permitted to the Communists abroad is that which finds expression in the telegrams of homage and addresses of thanks sent daily from all the world, including the Soviet Zone of Germany, to the Kremlin, messages fulsomely expressing gratitude to the wise leader and teacher Stalin and the great Russian people for their selfless friendship and guidance.

IV

What It All Means

*

Those, then, are the twelve links in the train of ideas that constitutes the Stalinist picture of history. The examples here given by way of illustration could be added to indefinitely; every new Soviet historical work, every new issue of *Voprossy Istorii*, supplies numbers of further evidences. But those already adduced may suffice. All the more so, since at about the same time an article appeared from the pen of a Marburg historian, Professor Dr. Georg von Rauch, "The fundamental lines of Soviet historiography under Stalinism". (*Europa-Archiv*, no. 5, pp. 19–21.) Dr. von Rauch's article gives an excellent, thorough chronological survey, forming a valuable addition to this essay. In particular the sections "Materials and problems of Soviet historiography, 1934–1945", and "Concluding remarks" contain a wealth of names and titles of works.

We were not concerned here to write the history of Soviet historiography, but to describe a state of things largely unknown in the world—in brief, the attempt to produce the world revolution by means of a new interpretation of world history—and then to ask, what does this state of things imply?

What does it mean in itself?

What It All Means

What does it mean for the Russians and the Soviet Union?

And what does it mean for Stalin?

To begin with, what does this state of things mean in itself?

FROM DIALECTIC TO MAGIC

Stalin's new historical doctrine means in the first place the destruction of Marxism as an absolute teaching of truth. The uniqueness of Bolshevism, together with the worldwide revolutionary movement it led, had consisted in the fact that Bolshevism rested on the broad and independent foundation of the teaching of Marx and Engels. The Bolsheviks were well aware of that fact. Not for nothing do they attach such immense importance to ideological indoctrination. Not for nothing do they subject the whole population to incessant ideological influencing through hundreds of thousands of trained propagandists and agitators. Not for nothing must everyone who wants to be anybody attend training courses, seminars, political colleges. This intellectual indoctrination, on which enormous energy is spent, took place in the dogma of Marx, Engels, and Lenin. It instructed the population, and especially the men and women in positions of responsibility, in the "iron laws" which Marx had proclaimed for the future of mankind.

All that has changed, and there is little doubt that it was Stalin who produced the change. In our frequent use of the words "Stalin" and "Stalinism" we have not employed them on the lines of the frequent use, for instance, of "Downing Street" for England. In 1934 it could only be guessed whether it was Stalin whose initiative was responsible for the decree on the teaching of history. Today we know that the driving force came from Stalin throughout this development. Between that decree of 1934 and the letters of 1950 on linguistics lies a whole series of measures of Stalin's that prove his great interest in that question. We may content ourselves here with categories, since in the essay referred to Dr. von Rauch gives the details.

Stalin himself took an interest in the drafts submitted for the new textbooks of history demanded in the decree of May 16th, 1934, and subjected them in August of the same year to sharp criticism. In April, 1936, he returned to the question of the teaching of history on the occasion of the award of a prize for a textbook for the third and fourth classes of the secondary schools. The manuscript of the first volume of the history of the civil war was closely examined by Stalin and given numbers of corrections. It was said at first that the "History of the Communist party of the Soviet Union", published in 1938, had been inspired by Stalin; it is now said that it was written by him. Since the appearance of that work it has been clear that Stalin took special interest in questions of historiography, and at every opportunity he is honoured as the "creator of Soviet historical research". In retrospect it can be seen that even long before 1934 Stalin's intellectual development showed traces of his later view of history.

Marx relativised

Taken together, all these decrees, articles, books, and

letters of Stalin's form the basis of the new Bolshevik historical doctrine, and that historical doctrine has destroyed the unity of the Marxist picture of the world. That fact did not become evident at once, since for a long time the inner breach was glossed over. But the time came when that was no longer possible, and Stalin found himself compelled to supply a clarification. This was provided in the fifth letter on linguistics, which Stalin wrote on July 28th, 1950, and which was published in *Pravda* on August 2nd.

In that letter Stalin mentions that Marx and Engels had no faith in the possibility of establishing Socialism in a single country, whereas the development in the Soviet Union· had proved the possibility of doing so. Stalin further points out that Engels wrote of the probability of the dying out of the State after the victory of the Socialist revolution, whereas the "Soviet Marxists of our day" came to the conclusion that even "the country of the successful Revolution" has need for a State of its own. Stalin is entirely right when he adduces as an example his claim of the "possibility of Socialism in a single country". In that claim lies the nucleus of his whole further intellectual development, of his development beyond Marx. The "learned in the Scriptures and Talmudists", he continues, stumble over these contradictions and imagine that only the one view or the other can be right. But they are just scriptural scholars and Talmudists, pettifoggers who "cannot penetrate into the heart of the matter". Stalin declares that "both conclusions are correct, but neither is absolute; each is correct for its own time".

What does it mean? It means nothing more or less

than that Marx and Engels are dethroned as teachers of the absolute truth, that they have been relativised, that their laws are no longer "iron", no longer valid once for all, but "each in its own time".

A relativised Marxism, however, can no longer be a dogma, and if Marxism is no longer a dogma—how can the individual Bolshevik know what he has to hold to?

What would remain of the Roman Catholic hierarchy if the Pope set out to relativise Saint Augustine, still more the New Testament? And what becomes of Bolshevik indoctrination if there is no longer any unambiguous Marxist dogma? What becomes of the "monolithic" following of the party?

Anyone who writes as Stalin wrote in that fifth letter finds himself in dangerous intellectual difficulties; he is leading the way from the epoch of the unambiguous dogma, binding on all the world, into the age of sophistry.

And that in its turn has consequences of the widest range. For in relativising Marxism Stalin relativises himself. So long as Marx and his iron laws were absolutes, anyone who applied those laws had a share in the absolute. But if Marx becomes relative, everything becomes relative. Everything—including the thoughts and actions of Marx's successor on the Marxist papal throne.

Thus Stalin's letters, which began as an attack on Marr, end with the dethronement of Marx.

This, too, has far-reaching consequences.

Marx owed his effectiveness to his inexorable logic. His appeal was to the human reason, the human capacity of seeing the general in the particular and of placing the general above the particular.

Lenin owed his effectiveness to the ruthless practical application of that logic in the transformation of a vast realm.

Stalin, however, appeals to the Russian's need for magic, to his readiness to be a missionary for his faith in salvation. In place of the iron laws (to which the Russian people would have to be subject if they really were iron laws), and in place of dialectics, Stalin introduces— national psychology.

This was not the result of a caprice of Stalin's: far from it. Marxism and Stalinism are mutually interdependent. The German people's journey from Liebknecht to Hitler, and the Russian people's journey from Lenin to Stalin, were parallel performances of the same process. In both cases, and for the same reason, the journey was one from dialectic to magic. Marx had suppressed every element of the subjective. But the subjective had not gone out of existence. Now it forced its way powerfully into the foreground. In the Soviet Union it calls itself Russian, the Russian Soviet man, the saviour of the world. Marxism was so abstract, so cold, so divested of all account of man and his emotional world, that there came into existence an icy psychological vacuum, into which inevitably, as a natural necessity there came one day the glow of a missionary idea, accompanied by a screeching hiss of suction.

Doctrine of the active superstructure

For the trained theorist that Stalin is, it is not enough to switch over more and more from dialectic to magic.

He must gain a theoretical grasp of the change and the reason for it, also subjecting the Marxist principle of the superstructure to thoroughgoing revision.

To Marx—and, till now, also to all his successors—the material basis was the primary element, and the superstructure the secondary element, dependent on the basis. The basis was for Marx the dog that wagged the superstructure. Regarded from the Marxist point of view, Stalin is making the tail wag the dog. In Stalin's first letter on linguistics, some little way from the beginning, there is the following paragraph:

"The superstructure is created by the basis. But that does not by any means imply that the superstructure merely reflects the basis, that it is passive and neutral and remains indifferent to the fate of its basis, to the fate of the classes, to the character of the social structure. On the contrary, once the superstructure has come into existence, it becomes the most powerful force, and then it actively assists its basis in forming and strengthening itself; then it undertakes all the measures for assisting the new social structure to destroy and liquidate the old basis and the old classes."

This doctrine of the active superstructure is regarded as so important that it was put forward once more at length in the *Pravda* article, already mentioned, of October 5th, 1950, "On the basis and the superstructure", in which the passage just quoted was reprinted with the following introductory note: "The inspired master of dialectics, Comrade Stalin, has revealed (*raskruil*) in his works on philological questions with special force the enormous active part of the superstructure in the life of society." G. Glezeman writes in a similar sense in a 16-page article, "Marxism-Leninism on basis and superstructure", in *Bolshevik* (1950, no. 18). The doctrine of the active rôle of the superstructure is thus expressly hailed as a discovery of Stalin's, and it is thus admitted without ado that Stalin has advanced in this point far beyond the doctrines of Marx and Engels.

Advanced—whither?

If we regard Fascism as one of the political forms of the twentieth century, Stalinism is today nearer to Fascism than to Marxism. The present essay should have shown this if nothing else.

THE PRACTICAL APPLICATION

What does this mean for the Russians, for the Soviet people? To understand that, we must bear in mind that the development of the view of history here described is not merely a matter for historians, ideologues, and other theorists. It has an eminently practical import-ance, and has influenced every field of Soviet life. At first it did so only gradually. At first the world war presented a crucial test of the Stalinist historiography. Today we know that the mental attitude it had spread contributed substantially to the turn in Stalin's favour in the Second World War.

Certainly nothing so stimulated the outburst of patriotism in the war years as the conduct of the Germans under Hitler's orders in the occupied regions of the U.S.S.R. But this would not alone have been enough; there had to be channels along which the Russian's fury and exasperation could flow. And these channels had been provided by the new historical doctrine. It had revealed *rodina*, the Russian fatherland, as the receptacle in which human progress was contained from the beginning of time. In these Messianic *rodina* emotions all the hatred of the intruders concentrated into an enormous force.

There had been some German observers, of course, who had been drawing attention to these developments since 1934. But in Germany (as in the rest of the world) people were so full of the ideas they had formed of Bolshevism in the first years after the Revolution that no attention was paid to the possibility of its fundamental modification, so that people were completely unprepared for the spectacle of the events of the late autumn of 1941.

The Guards on the march

On November 11th, 1941, in the midst of the most disastrous rearguard fighting, Stalin signed a decree: "For heroic conduct and brave fighting on the battlefield against the Germans, the Fourteenth Tank Brigade is awarded the title of First Tank Brigade of Guards." That was the starting-point for a long series of measures adopted during the years that followed in order to raise the fighting spirit of the Soviet troops by the restoration of old Russian military traditions. The Guards had been so called in the past because they were entrusted as a bodyguard with the special protection of the Tsar and the dynasty. The troops of the Guards, and especially the officers of the Guards, in the old army were thus the most hated enemies of the Bolsheviks, and many of them lost their lives at the hands of Bolsheviks for no other reason than their membership of a regiment of the Guards. Now, however, all that was forgotten. The Russian soldiers of 1941 were deliberately associated with those of the Tsarist past. "Glorious were the old Russian Guards. They were in Berlin and Leipzig and Paris. They died in the battles of the [first] world war." (*Pravda*, December 15th, 1941.)

An old officer of the Tsarist Guards who was still living, A. Ignatiev, was raked up to write for the Soviet soldiers' newspapers sentences like this: "The Guards die, but they never surrender. We old officers of the Russian Guards, who lived through the wars of the past, are doubly fortunate in finding that the best deeds of heroism of the Guards in our history are not only being continued by the warriors of the Red Army but are being outdone by them. Great was the heroism of the old Russian Guards! They came into existence under the command of that great Russian war lord Peter the Great, after the temporary defeat at Narva, and they covered themselves with undying glory in the victory at Poltava. Their banners and standards bore the traces of German, French, and Turkish shot. Whole generations of warriors were trained in their fighting tradition. Many members of the old Guards have the great honour of standing today in the ranks of the command of our glorious Red Army."

Orders and epaulettes

On July 29th, 1942, came another Stalin decree: three new Soviet orders were created, named after Suvorov, Kutusov, and Alexander Nevsky. What had those three men to do with the Soviet régime? Suvorov and Kutusov were highly unrevolutionary generals of the eighteenth and nineteenth centuries, pious Orthodox Christians, loyal servants of their Tsars, by whom, in recognition of their faithful service, they were raised to princely rank. Both were typical representatives of Tsarism, and Suvorov led some of his campaigns against the Russian rebels under the popular leader Pugachev, whom the Bolsheviks regard as one of their Russian forerunners. Alexander Nevsky had been a thirteenth-century Grand Duke, a member of the Russian ruling house; he is revered by the Orthodox Church as one of its saints. These three figures are embodiments of all that the Bolsheviks had opposed and condemned in the first years of their rule. Now they had to give these three names to the highest orders in the Red Army. In the form of those orders, too, the association between Russian history and the Bolshevik present was to be given visible expression. In the Order of Suvorov the medallion of the old general is surrounded by the five-point star of the Bolsheviks; in the Order of Kutusov a tower of the Kremlin is to be seen behind the marshal's head, but above it is not the Tsarist double eagle but the five-point star; and among the symbols of the Order of Alexander Nevsky, alongside the old warrior's battle-axe, are the hammer and sickle.

On January 10th, 1943, under a decree of the Supreme Soviet, the same epaulettes were introduced for the Red Army which twenty-six years earlier had been torn from the uniforms of Tsarist officers. Under decrees of the Supreme Soviet of July 9th and August 11th, 1943, the officers' ranks which in the past had been abolished with contumely were restored in the Red Army.

What It All Means

On December 20th, 1943, Stalin presented to the Soviet people a new national anthem, a condensation of his messianic-patriotic historical doctrine. The anthem seeks to put into words what the orders inculcated pictorially, the union of the Russian element with the Bolshevik, even at the price of the rhyming, almost an indignity to Russian ears, of Rus' (the name of the mediaeval State of Kiev) with Sovietskyi Soyuz ("Soviet Union").

The course and the end of the war between Hitler and Stalin showed that these things were more than silly trivialities. They had a profound influence on the events of those years. They made Stalingrad possible. Their effect is continuing after the war. Stalin's letters of the summer of 1950 on linguistics were needed to confirm once more the line started on in 1934 and continued through the war.

New—or age-old?

Is it, indeed, a new line? one might ask. Is it not really an age-old line, proceeding from the remote depths of Russian history? Does it not lead from Ilarion's teaching (in the eleventh century) of the special blessedness of the Russian people, past the idea of the Third Rome (about 1500), past the emperor Paul's conviction that he had been chosen to be the new Saint George in the struggle against the Antichrist Bonaparte, past the dreams of Alexander I and the claim of Nicholas I to be the Gendarme of Europe, past Leontiev, past Dostoevsky's "Every man must first become Russian", to the gospel of the Communist International? Did not people talk during Napoleon's campaign of the Russian's "Scythian tactics"? Did not Lomonossov, in the eighteenth century, attack the Norman theory, which offended his national pride as a Russian? Was not the authoritative influence of Byzantium belittled (for instance, by Prisselkov) even before the First World War? And did not the revision of the assessment of Ivan the Terrible begin with Kisevetter's book as early as 1898?

To all this the only possible reply is: Yes, there has been all that and much more. (Professor Martin Winkler has given a comprehensive account of the forerunners of the Stalinist idea of a mission in a work shortly to appear, *Vom Wesen des Russischen Menschen*.) The Stalinist view of history owes, indeed, part of its effectiveness among the Russians to the circumstance that it corresponds much more closely to the Russian tradition and to Russian aspirations than such unflattering treatment of Russianism as was contained in Pokrovsky's historical teaching or Marr's philology. Here, too, lies the explanation—apart from the terrorism that overwhelms every dweller in the Soviet realm afresh every day—of the fact that among others even the Soviet historians of the older generation have largely placed their talents in the service of the elaboration of the new doctrine.

And yet there is a great difference between the development that extended from Ilarion to Dostoevsky and the development since 1934. What was to be found in the past in the visions of individual seers or in the works of individual scholars, has now been co-ordinated and fused into a regular educational system with a solid structure, compelling universal unconditional acceptance, a system continually provided with new and stiffer "corset ribs" by periodisation. A gigantic ideological edifice is under construction, and hundreds, if not thousands, of historians, archivists, archaeologists, ethnographers, linguists, sociologists, economists, authors, art historians, and philologists are working day and night to complete it.

Unadmitted change

Does this exhaust the consequences to the Russians of Stalin's new historical doctrine? By no means. Let us picture the violent alternations that have been imposed on the Russians in the course of a single generation: within a few years they have been plunged from the thin air of ice-cold dialectic into the oppressive heat of a gospel of salvation by magic.

Well, other peoples have been put through all sorts of experiences in recent decades. But the special feature of the development in the U.S.S.R. lies in the fact that this change was carried out under the same banner of the same Bolshevism, and that a daily propaganda through millions of sheets seeks to demonstrate to the people (and to the world) that the same Stalin who today is lord over the life and death and ideology of two hundred million Soviet citizens was from the first the most intimate adviser and colleague of Lenin; that there has thus been no change at all; that on the contrary an absolutely straight line runs from Marx via Lenin to Stalin.

It is all too obvious that this cannot be so, and the fact cannot fail to be realised by the Russian. Certainly his lords and masters do everything they can to give him no opportunity to think about it. They set him galloping, with his tongue hanging out, from one five-year plan to the next, although the faith in the panacea of a five-year plan, which was strong and genuine under the first plan, has long since given place to a resigned disillusion. The men in the Kremlin make demands from him such as were never made of any people, except of the Germans by Hitler in the last years of the war—and that has now been going on for thirty years. Again and again the people pull themselves together under the promises of a better future, amid the terrorism of an unexampled police State. One after another of their essential qualities was mobilised by Stalin and thrown into his struggle for world domination. Their intellect, their love of their country, the missionary zeal and readiness for sacrifice that slumber in the depths of their soul, and their religious feeling. In every way they were made to serve Stalin's purpose.

Will not the Russian one day realise with horror that all the sacred objects in whose name his masters have driven him into the utmost exertions mean nothing to those masters, that they "inject" them into him just as if they were pervitin or some other drug for driving men from one peak to the next? Since 1945 the Russian people has been able to realise that Stalin's appeals to national feeling, with which he urged on the people during the war, were after all not so genuine as to be able to bring the people a better existence. Everything very quickly became as before, when there were no regiments of the Guards and no Orders of Saint Alexander Nevsky.

And as for the glorification of the Russian people and its history, the Russian will be bound to discover one day that, in proportion as Russian history is turned by the efforts of the Soviet historians into world history, the Russian people will lose its own history in the ocean of world historiography.

Growing isolation

The Russian will also realise with alarm the growing isolation in which he is set in consequence of Stalin's new doctrine. It separates the Russian from all the rest of mankind. The days are over when a Russian was received as a comrade and brother at radical workers' demonstrations from the Ruhr to Yokohama. Today he is the feared precursor of the taskmaster of tomorrow. The days are over when Russian revolutionary literature was scattered throughout the world. Today it is as wearying and lifeless in its monotonous description of the Russian superman as the monumentally exaggerated descriptions in the Third Reich of Germanic virtues. Russian scientists are now scarcely seen at congresses abroad; and where they do appear, they pass their days in the ghetto of the Muscovite regulations that impose on them a language that convinces no one. The same Russians whom the Kremlin tries to persuade that they are the leaders of the world and the quintessence of world history, the heirs and representatives of all that was valuable in the development of the West since Hellas and Rome, are compelled to turn away from the West with a violence unparalleled since the sanguinary dealings of Peter the Great with the Russian isolationists of his time.

Through this attitude, through the agitation against any sort of contact between the Soviet citizen and the Western world, against "cosmopolitan spittle-licking and obeisances to the West", through the persecution of all who give the slightest hint that there is anything good in the West, or admit any Russian "borrowing" from the West, the Kremlin is driving the population of the Soviet Union into a disastrous isolationism. In so doing it not only condemns to extinction a great deal that was really great and fine in Russian history and civilisation, but destroys the bases of further intellectual and scientific progress among the Russians, to whom all fruitful contact with foreign countries is prohibited as high treason. Here laws come into play that lie far outside all the Marxian dialectic, laws such as that a messianic doctrine of salvation, calling for the conversion of the whole world, inevitably leads to isolation, intolerance, and loneliness.

THE CHOSEN PEOPLE AND THE OTHERS

All this, positive and negative, is implied for the Russians and the U.S.S.R. in Stalin's revision of Marxism. And what does it imply for the rest of the world? It implies simply the rejection of the solidarity of the international proletariat. Stalin's new gospel makes demands not only on the Russians but on the rest of the world, demands which in the long run the latter will not tolerate.

With the "iron laws" of Marx, applicable to everything and everybody, it was possible to accumulate a worldwide following. But how will that following be held together under the doctrine that the Russians are the Chosen People?

Since the introduction of the metric system, all

measurements have been made in metres (even though some peoples continue to use other measures among themselves); similarly the history of mankind is in future to be measured by the standard of Soviet history. That is the purpose of the Stalinist historiography, even though the Soviet ideologues would have to reject that comparison. They would say that it was a more or less arbitrary proceeding to make the metre equivalent to the forty-millionth part of the circumference of the earth; after all, the fifty-millionth part might just as well have been chosen. But, they will say, Russian and Soviet history does not owe its rôle as a measure of world history to a chance. At that point, it is true, further questions would seriously embarrass them. If it is not due to chance, to what *is* it due? Here lies the limit of a system of ideas that makes use of metaphysics and at the same time rejects metaphysics.

The appeal to the belief that the Russian people are a Chosen People has fallen on fruitful soil among the Russians. But what about the other peoples of the world?

In the epoch of the Roman Empire the historical consciousness of most peoples was so little developed that they made no objection to the imposition upon them of Rome's picture of her history. In the middle of the twentieth century, however, the position is not the same. It is highly improbable that a conception built up entirely on Russian and Soviet history can be imposed on other peoples. Even in the U.S.S.R., where people have no defence against the Bolshevik ideologues, the effectiveness of the new theories diminishes with distance from the Great Russians, and grows again only along the periphery of the country, where it is addressed to primitive peoples without a developed historical consciousness of their own.

World patriotism=world imperialism

The weakness of the theory outside the U.S.S.R. was shown by the conflict with Tito. What happened was like the story of the emperor's clothes. At the imperial court everyone was quite ready to believe that his eyes were deceiving him when he saw the emperor with nothing on. But when a man appeared who knew nothing of court etiquette and had the courage and the simplicity to say: "Why, the man's naked", the scales fell from the eyes of the others. Similarly Tito said: "Why, that's not international patriotism, but a grandiose imperialism, setting out to harness the peoples of the world to its chariot"—and suddenly countless people all over the world agreed with him.

Stalin's arguments collapse when they are really countered. Provided, it is true, that they are countered with energy and self-confidence. The new historical doctrine—and not only that but Bolshevism as a whole —is based on the need of the weak for something to lean on, that is to say of those who are unable to rise as individuals against their past (economic and political) masters, and who think they can do it with Stalin's help, without noticing that then they exchange a rod for a cat-o'-nine-tails. Stalinism addresses itself to all who want someone else to lay down the law for them because they cannot do it for themselves, and who are ready to be immersed in the great sea of Slavdom. Even in Asia, where the sins of colonial imperialism are exacting a bitter penalty, and where every hand that claims to be "anti-imperialist" is clutched, opposition against the domination of Moscow will grow with the increasing recognition of Moscow's true nature. And in Europe? Here every Communist is a latent Titoist, once he has realised the real meaning of Stalinism.

Whether we call it dialectics or not, as surely as Robespierre gave place to a Napoleon and Marx produced a Stalin, so Stalinism was bound to give birth to Titoism.

It is not intended to put forward here the all too simple contention that patriotism of the Stalinist type is nothing but a resurrection of the patriotism of the time of the Tsars. Anyone who thinks—and there are many who do, including some leading American publicists and politicians—that the Russians are simply continuing today to carry out the pan-Russian expansion which the Revolution had compelled the Tsars to stop, is taking too simple a view of developments. The new expression coined by the Soviets, "international patriotism", paradoxical as it seems at first sight, has its justification. In consequence of the many peoples within the frontiers of the Tsarist empire, the old patriotism of the Russians was stretched farther than that of the French or Germans, but the present patriotism is stretched incomparably farther. The patriotism of the Russians oscillates between the poles of the Russian *rodina* and a worldwide *patria*. Stalin is trying to hammer into them the conviction that everything that serves the advance and the power of the Soviet Union also serves the true interests of mankind. Thus there comes into existence a world patriotism that is scarcely distinguishable from world imperialism.

Finally, what does the propagation of the new view of history mean for Stalin himself?

We must not take too simple a view of the matter and say, for instance, that Marx went to work only with dialectics and the intellect and Stalin only with the appeal to faith, with magic. As regards Marx, that simple statement may serve, but with Stalin the position is more complicated. To read his speeches and writings is to gain the impression of two souls beneath a single breast. In Stalin dialectical training and the Marxist dogma which ten thousand repetitions have made part of his flesh and blood, are in conflict with the recognition, gradually increasing through many years, that in this world there are not only subjects of economic laws of development, but also personal and national individualities.

In times of crisis the normal human being is inclined to be guided less by the promptings of his intellect than by those of his feelings, his instinct, his experience—in brief, what his nose tells him.

In the times of supreme danger, in the years 1941–1943, Stalin had experience of the vast sources of power available to him in the Russian people if he addressed himself to their "Russian soul". It is also no mere chance that the first Stalin letter on linguistics appeared in *Pravda* on June 20th, 1950, five days before the outbreak of the Korean war, that is to say at a time when the "cold war" was rapidly coming to a climax; the letters on linguistics, with their shrill reminder of the continually victorious course of the Russian language, were an attempt, at a time of grave international crisis, to go down to the root of the matter, to return to the origin of the two sources of Russian power—if they had not gradually dried up through perpetual misuse. Nor was it mere chance that Stalin, of whose private life and family circumstances not a word has ever reached the public, shortly after his first evocation of the past in the decreeing of the new historical doctrine, actually made a journey, carefully and industriously publicised in the press, to his mother in the Caucasus. Until that day not a man in Russia had known whether Stalin's mother was still alive.

What Stalin wants is the domination of Bolshevism over the world; he wants his own domination over the world. Probably this effort to rule the world is adorned in his head with the idea that in so doing he would be serving the world. Throughout his whole intellectual past, Marxism was to him the first instrument and the nearest at hand for attaining that aim. In proportion as Marxism proved inadequate, he added another instrument to it. There is much to show that he is well aware of the inner conflicts thus produced, especially of the really hectic form of agitation continually pursued throughout the country in the effort to reconcile Stalinism with Marxism, making use of the trick of describing everything that will not fit into the Stalinist system, such as the works of Pokrovsky, as "popular Marxism".

Perhaps it would be better, in our technical age, to

speak not of two souls but of two motors. When his Marxist motor no longer gave efficient service in his aeroplane, Stalin had a second one built in, magical-messianic. At first it did in fact give greater speed, astonishing the world in 1942–1943. But every technician knows that in the long run everything depends on the two working with the same rhythm, because otherwise there is a danger that the machine may break up in the air. Who could guarantee Stalin's two motors in that respect?

"Look at the contradictions in the West: they will smash it!" So Moscow shouts to us every day. There certainly are plenty of contradictions in the West, and over against them, till now, stood Marxism as a consistent system. But it does so no longer. The contradictions within Bolshevism are manifest. The naïve self-confidence with which the Soviet peoples marched into a future dictated by Stalin will one day be destroyed by those contradictions.

In that lies the true significance of Stalin's historical doctrine.